Keys for Church Growth

KEYS
for Church
Growth

by
Louie E. Bustle

Beacon Hill Press of Kansas City
Kansas City, Missouri

Contents

Introduction

Pastors are asking, "How can my church grow?" Indeed, all pastors need to ask this question if the soul-winning business is to go forward. While thankfully many are asking the question, few are finding answers. Pastors who continue to ask become frustrated because they cannot find ways to grow the local church.

There is a key to each church; it is available, and the pastor can find it! But he cannot be satisfied with his church if it has "a form of godliness, but denying the power thereof" (2 Tim. 3:5). Those who are in the church must regain a genuine concern for the lostness of man in sin. Then in the power of the Spirit the church can offer man the cure for his problems.

Many pastors are saying, "I have done all I can; help me!" For this reason I am presenting these church growth principles, philosophies, and methodologies. May they fan a spark of action and encourage everyone who is serious about his calling. Although I am not an authority in the field of church growth, these ideas come from years of studying, watching, discussing, and from personal experiences in planting the church. These are ideas and concepts that have worked. If you will contextualize them, you will find that many of them will work for you.

This book does not consider the organizational structure of the church. Its purpose is to present concepts of church growth with the pastor in mind. Their use is always a personal thing. Organize your people to *go, share,* and *bring people to Jesus.* Only then can they be effective members of the church.

Pastors study but do nothing about what they have

learned. Instead, they accumulate plans to help the church get out of its rut and grow. Be willing to develop an innovative strategy for growth in his church.

So much good material on church growth is being published today that you can easily use the ideas of others to help grow your church. Expertise of others is a valuable resource, and these books are excellent supplements to your study on the subject. You will learn from the proven successes and failures of others and not waste your time trying the wrong strategies.

One of the greatest study resources is the Word of God. There we find examples that work in today's world. The Bible is still relevant concerning church growth. It inspires people to see the responsibility and privilege of making the church grow.

The population is growing at a faster rate than the church. The church needs a system of growth to accomplish the task of evangelizing the world for God. Slow growth will not do it! A system of church growth must cover all aspects of the church, from the training of pastors to the mobilization of the laity. We need a system of organization that involves everyone all of the time. Church growth cannot depend on one person to do all of the work. The pastor inspires the people, trains them for the task, and coordinates them as the team grows the church.

1

The Pastor and God's Plan
for Church Growth

God's plan for the world is wrapped up in a statement of Jesus to Peter in Matt. 16:18: "I will build my church." This declaration is the fulfillment of the promise of God to Abraham in the Old Testament. God wanted His name to be known in all the nations, but Israel failed to fulfill this mission.[1] Jesus did not mean that He alone was going to build His Church. God's plan was for Jesus to go back to the Father so that He could send the Holy Spirit to the world to convict the sinner and convince, guide, and fill the believer.

God chose people in His Church to share a great part of the responsibility of building the Church. He has entrusted the gospel to humans who are filled with His Spirit. What a privilege in these last days to be a part of God's plan for the world. He is "not willing that any should perish, but that all should come to repentance" (2 Pet. 3:9).

At the same time we must remember that the growth of the church is neither human nor secular. Although there are favorable conditions that the pastor helps create, and methodologies that advance his efforts toward reaching the goal of church growth, without Christ as the Builder, the results are only numbers, philosophies, and methodologies. Christ must build His Church! He goes before. He goes after. He goes with everyone. Christ can work without us, but most of the time He chooses to work through us to reach the world. Can we fail in the commission to build His Church?

We go in the authority of Jesus Christ. After His resurrection, Jesus announced to His disciples in Matt. 28:18 that "all power" was placed in His control. In verses 19-20 He imparts the Great Commission: "Go ye therefore, and teach all nations, baptizing them in the name of the Father, and of the Son, and of the Holy Ghost: teaching them to observe all things whatsoever I have commanded you: and, lo, I am with you alway, even unto the end of the world." Then He commissioned His disciples to share in the authority of Christ. "This established authority, designed to have positive effects, is exercised by pastors and leaders of the congregation by solemn charge from God."[2] That charge in Acts 20:28 says: "Be on guard for yourselves and for all the flock, among which the Holy Spirit has made you overseers, to shepherd the church of God which He purchased with His own blood" (NASB).

God wills that His Church grow. The pastor is the key person in the growing church. Almost all churches, if we will strive to do all we can to create the right conditions, with God's power, will grow. With God on our side, we cannot lose. The destiny of the church can be changed with God's help. Are we willing to be used to build His Church?

If this is true, what are you doing to help your church grow? God has a plan for each pastor's ministry and his people. Primarily, God wants the church to be *a spiritual center.* It is not a club or a social group. The church is a fueling station, where believers go to be encouraged, to study the Word of God, to be injected with power, and to mature in living as well as witnessing. It is a center for sharing burdens with one another and leaving them at the Cross. There the sinner can find pardon from his sins. The church is a powerful force in worship and evangelism.

Overcoming Obstinate Obstacles

During my teaching experience, one young, energetic, prospective pastor asked a valid question: How can a church grow if the leaders and many members are carnal? Another student wanted to know how to grow a church if the members do not want to grow. There are no simple answers to either of these questions.

The church belongs to God. There is always a key! If the church is carnal, one draws it to Christ by the Word. A good foundation precedes solid progress. You can build a strong biblical foundation and have good church growth simultaneously. A healthy church produces healthy fruit. Careful planning and preaching can change the nature of the church.

But if the people of the church appear to lack the desire to grow, we need to get back to the basics. The spiritual emphasis is the best approach. When the hearts of the people are right, growth can be promoted. The church can be like a child who is not growing. The problem may be not growth but nurture. When the child eats a well-balanced diet, he will feel like exercising. As he does, he will begin to grow naturally. Spiritual motivation fosters the desire that is needed in the heart of each Christian to help the church grow.

If the old church is not willing to grow, win a "new" church. You can go to the street, knock on doors, and present the gospel. If you can win 20 people the first year and train them, you will have a new church the next year. New people put life into the "old" church. It becomes a spiritual center, which is attractive to others.

The world will never be won for Christ unless the Spirit-filled Christians multiply, and centers of evangelism are multiplied and established all over the world. Each church can start another church. This creates enthusiasm and unity in the mother church. The mother church is the hen that rallies and protects her baby chicks. As they grow up and leave the mother hen, each new generation rears its own group of chicks. That is multiplication.

Applying that principle to the church, if the church becomes a mother church by giving birth to at least 1 more, then each of them gives birth to 1 more, that makes 4; then 8, 16, 32, 64; and soon reproduction does not have to take place only in the city of that local church. Church planters and missionaries can be sent to plant the church in other areas, sometimes even into other countries.

There is a desperate need for the planting of churches all over the world. There are millions of people in the world and only a small percentage are professing to be born again. If 10 denominations were to plant even 100 churches per year, Jesus would never win the world. A faster method of winning the world is for each church to reproduce itself every year.

The Lord will lead you in every aspect of planning for church growth. By the end of this study, you will be able to develop a plan for reproducing the church and its membership. Organization, time, and effort are required to reach the goal the Lord will lay upon your heart.

God wants His Church to be a church in mission. There is something exciting about putting others first. It is a principle that works not only in the lives of individuals but also in the life of the collective body of Christ's Church. As Christians put others first, God helps them in their work close at home. When Paul learned to decrease, God's work increased. To lean on the Lord and be dependent on Him always brings strength and power.

God blesses the members as they have faith and as they work to help the church grow. Faith is an element that baffles non-Christians, but the Christian understands it as he walks with the Lord. Faith stretches as one puts others first. It takes faith to divide a Sunday School class, or a church, and wait to see growth take place. It takes faith to give sacrificially and expect God to make the church grow. This is all in God's biblical plan for building His Church.

God calls everyone to build the Kingdom. Some naturally have different gifts and callings, but God's plan is for everyone to do something in His Church. Isaiah received a call from God and responded, "Here am I; send me" (6:8). It is vitally important to possess that call, especially when the going gets rough. But what can the church and pastor do to get leaders?

God always calls pastors and leaders to carry on His work in His Church. You, the pastor, play an important part in this. You have to create the right conditions so that your people can clearly hear God talking to them. They need to know God wants to use them. The job of the pastor is to train them, provide opportunities for them to serve, and guide them to be open to the Holy Spirit and His leadership.

Some have the idea that only the most "super" intelligent or talented pastors can have good church growth. That is not true. Although the pastor needs the ability to plan and think and organize people, God can take all abilities and use them to help the work grow. If the pastor lacks certain abilities, he can surround himself with others to make up for his shortcomings. Each pastor needs to know his own weaknesses so that he can choose strong leaders especially in these areas.

When God calls a person to the ministry, he has to come to the place of complete surrender to the will of God to preach the gospel. That call should enable him to evangelize better. It is true that the pastor needs to catch a vision of the lost going to hell to wake him up to the great need for the church to grow. Understandably he preaches Christ because He loved and changed him. He wants to obey Christ's calling and will be motivated to a positive overflow of love from the heart. Paul summed it up when he said, "Woe is unto me, if I preach not the gospel!" (1 Cor. 9:16).

Training Leaders

As pastor you will learn to recognize and train leaders. Paul Orjala derives from Donald McGavran five classes of church leaders, all of which are necessary, but church growth goes forward only as these are kept in balance.

Class One leaders serve inside the church— church officers, board members, Sunday School teachers, choir members, committee members, and others.

Class Two leaders are volunteer workers who serve outside the church in outreach ministries to non-Christians in visitation evangelism and personal evangelism. They may at the same time double as Class One leaders.

Class Three leaders are leaders of small groups. They may be volunteers or partially paid, and they serve as leaders of Bible study groups, task force ministries to special groups, house churches, and the like.

Class Four leaders are the full-time, paid leaders of congregations, such as pastors and full-time staff members.

Class Five leaders are the superintending and motivating leaders who travel beyond the local church, such as district and denominational leaders.[3]

So many times the pastor wants church growth because he feels pressure from leaders in authority. He in turn applies pressure to *make* the church grow. Growth does not usually happen this way.

The inspiration for church growth must come through the work of the Holy Spirit in the lives of the pastor and people. There are many ideas and plans for church growth, but no plan is valid unless it is woven within the context of the Word of God. The Word is the authority that is necessary for solid numerical and spiritual growth. In the Word we find beautiful examples of growth that can help us. The Church grew explosively as we see it in Acts 2. Also, Paul had marvelous growth in part because of his prolific use the Word. Help will come when the pastor goes to the Word of God.

God's plan for all leaders is to reproduce themselves. First, the pastor should look for new workers from whom he can reproduce himself with another pastor. Lay workers should also be trained to involve others in the work by training, motivating, and reproducing themselves. This is the only way the church can be assured of making a great impact on the world.

God's plan for believers is to support church growth. There are at least three ways people can do this. The first is through doing. A team plays ball together, or it will not be a team. If the whole church is working, then the work will be accomplished more rapidly as well as more efficiently. The people have to forget the idea that the pastor is trained and therefore the only one who can do the work. Everyone can be a worker for growing the church.

The second way to support church growth is through financial giving. Everyone can participate in this means of support. Without the tithe the church struggles to pay the local bills with little left for outreach. Too many times funds are inadequate to pay the pastor. Churches should be taught to support the pastor well. Offerings of love should be given above the tithe in order that God's church can march to victory and growth.

The third method of supporting church growth is by prayer. Prayer is so important that it cannot be over-emphasized. The time spent in prayer is directly proportional to church growth. When prayers increase, the church grows, especially if the other conditions are met. The pastor needs to start groups praying for his church now!

"The congregation should be so structured that it encourages mobilization of the people to be a *gathered* people, a group called out from the world to worship God and to edify one another, and to be the *scattered* people, a group going out into the world to confess Christ. This is the divine rhythm of the church's life: Come and go, gather and scatter."[4]

In many churches there is a one-sided emphasis: "Come." The doors of the church are opened, saying, "World, come on in." But the world does not enter, and the church wonders why. Since Israel failed similarly in her responsibility to take God's message to the nations, God sent a new Israel, the Church, to go and proclaim. This Church is not only to say, "Come," but also to go. "But ye shall receive power, after that the Holy Ghost is come upon you: and ye shall be witnesses unto me both in Jerusalem, and in all Judaea, and in Samaria, and unto the uttermost part of the earth" (Acts 1:8). Paul Orjala in his classroom says, "The church always grows by recruitment."

Gifts for Growth

The Church of Jesus Christ is so designed for growth through the church that God gives each of His children gifts to aid them in the task. Misunderstandings abound today concerning spiritual gifts. They are *not* the fruit of the Spirit. "The fruit of the Spirit is love, joy, peace, patience, kindness, goodness, faithfulness, gentleness, self-control" (Gal. 5:22-23, NASB). They are *not* just talents or skills but God-given, God-chosen abilities that Jesus uses to build up the Church and fulfill its ministry in the world.

What are spiritual gifts, then? Four important concepts concerning gifts might help us at this point:

First, gifts are given for a purpose. They are not intended to be used for man's glory but for the glory of the Most High. Second, all God's people have gifts. No one is left out. Third, gifts are given by the Spirit as He chooses. Finally, all gifts have an interdependence and mutual ministry within the Church. It is like a good ball team—no one player can win a game without the help from the other members of that team.

Individual gifts are summarized as (1) prophecy, (2) service, (3) teaching, (4) exhortation, (5) giving, (6) leadership, and (7) mercy or compassion in Rom. 12:6-8. First Corinthians 12 gives a longer list: (1) wisdom, (2) knowledge, (3) faith, (4) healings, (5) miracles, (6) prophecy, (7) discernment, (8) languages, (9) interpretation, (10) helps, and (11) administrations.

Some Christians may receive several of these gifts. For example, all Christians have the responsibility of tithing, but some will have the gift of giving, which is also the ability to earn more money to be placed in the service of the Lord.

Dr. John A. Knight related this story to me. He met a millionaire who had been converted for two years. The man was excited about being a Christian. He told Dr. Knight, "I have this great desire to earn more money." Dr. Knight was curious to find out why. The man answered, "If I can make more money, I can give more money." All Christians are to be witnesses, but some will have the gift of evangelism. All should be winning people to Christ, but those who have the gift of evangelism can be effective on a broader scale.

Some of these gifts are lifelong endowments, while others are for a shorter time. Faith for healing can be given as a gift for a specific occasion, depending on the circumstances. No one has faith to heal everyone, but God gives faith for certain occasions.

Other gifts often mentioned are: (1) hospitality (1 Pet. 4:9-10)—church people need to welcome and talk to new people, making them feel comfortable in the church; (2) intercession—all of God's people need to be taught to be active in prayer if the church is to grow; (3) celibacy (1 Cor. 7:7); (4) voluntary poverty (13:3); and (5) martyrdom (v. 3).

How does one discover which spiritual gifts God has for him? Peter Wagner suggests five practical steps:

1. Explore the possibilities.
2. Experiment with as many as possible.
3. Examine his feelings.
4. Evaluate his effectiveness.
5. Expect confirmation from the body of Christ.

And we might add a sixth step of inner confirmation by God's Spirit, writes Paul Orjala.[5]

At times the pastor feels he cannot do the job without material equipment. It is very true that God does supply our every need but not always all of our desires. Many times better equipment may help the pastor do a better job. However, he must not set his sights on material gain, or he will be defeated in reaching his goals. In some countries, each pastor feels he must have a strong public-address system with loudspeakers on the outside of the church to preach effectively. It is true that the neighbors can also hear the message even though they are at home. Equipment is important, but the question is, where do the funds come from? Is there enough money to buy all of the equipment for potential Christian workers? No, not if all Christians are being effectively mobilized to evangelize.

The good news is that God is not dependent on things. He uses things and can supply them when He chooses. One great example of God miraculously supplying a need comes from the Virgin Islands. A few years ago, we were trying to purchase land to build a church building. The government had passed a law requiring two acres as a minimum area for building a church. The Lord had given us $7,000 for the land. After the new law was passed, there was no way to purchase the land with only $7,000. Two acres would have cost us $40,000. We began to pray and trust God for a miracle. God sent us a man who wanted to sell nine acres for $45,000, which was inexpensive but still not within our reach. When we talked with him, we discovered that he only wanted $7,000 as a down payment, and the remaining funds could be paid over a six-year period. This was just the amount that we had! We purchased it. Work began on the project with two acres set aside from the plot for the church. After building a road, the remaining lots were sold for a total of $72,000. You see, God is bigger than we think!

When we went to the Dominican Republic with the Jerry Porter family as pioneer missionaries, our goal was to begin 9 churches during the first year. We set a budget of $7,500 for the project of faith. When we received our funds, only $5,000 had been allotted. One of our pastors said to me, "We will just have to cut back on the number of churches we were going to start." I answered, "But where is faith? If God wanted us to start nine churches before, why would we let the budget stop our miracle-working God?" Actually at the end of the year, we had 12 new churches and a total of $8,000 was spent. God made up the difference from other sources. God does supply material needs when He desires.

In Acts 1:8 we find a victorious Christ who had completed His suffering of death on the Cross. He had accomplished His ministry here in the physical form. Now He continues to teach His own. Jesus was serious when He gave His last message to those early Christians, "Ye shall receive power"! This is not the power of the world but the power of the Holy Spirit working in the believers.

The Bible teaches there is power for the child of God to live without sin in his life. The Christian can be victorious in his day-by-day walk with Christ. That is the message. First John 1:7 tells us, "If we walk in the light, as he is in the light, we have fellowship one with another, and the blood of Jesus Christ his Son cleanseth us from all sin." The atonement for sin is complete. Anyone can receive the power over all sin by receiving the Holy Spirit into his heart. Maturity and growth follow by daily fellowship and walk with the Lord.

One purpose of this empowering of the Holy Spirit is not to sit but to share Christ. After receiving the fullness of the Holy Spirit, "You shall be My witnesses" (NASB). The church—not the building, but the people who are the body of Christ—has the privilege of taking the gospel into all the world.

What does witness mean? Elmer L. Towns wrote that the ministers of the 10 largest Sunday Schools "tend to reject the term *witness* in favor of the term *soul winning.*"[6] That witness means pressing the claims of the gospel to acquire a decision but also involves presence evangelism.

Presence evangelism is the opposite extreme from aggressive soul winning. Presence evangelism is letting one's life witness without a verbal proclamation or testimony. In some countries where it is prohibited by law to preach the gospel, presence evangelism may be the only form of witness. It may also be necessary where strong opposition to the church or its message exists. Its aim is that sooner or later people will make a decision to follow Christ.

Soul-winning witness is very important to help the church grow. Along with that emphasis one needs to know when to pull in the net. If the net is pulled in too soon or too quickly, the fish will take a path of retreat. If green fruit is picked too soon, it will spoil and is not useful to anyone.

Jesus promised in Matt. 28:20 that He will be with every believer. Being equipped with spiritual power and going in the presence of the Lord marks the success of any pastor as he does the work of the ministry. What confidence that gives us! As the Christian lives in the Spirit, he walks in the Spirit, and he witnesses in the Spirit. Christ is with him, driving out fear. With Christ's presence the mission of sharing the gospel can be done, and at the same time the pastor can equip the laity to do the work of ministry also.

Vision and Goals

A vision is the ability to imagine the possible future. A goal is set by the person who has a vision. Goals are methods or instructions for fulfilling a mission. The Lord can help us motivate our church to see a vision for the work, to see the possibilities for growth. God expects every pastor to pray for a vision of what God wants him to do. One man may see the possibility of a particular church reaching an attendance of 100 persons, while another may well see the possibility of reaching 1,000 people for the church. There will be different visions with some pastors bearing greater responsibilities. But what about the church? Is it just the pastor who is to have the vision? *No!* The whole church should seek the vision for its ministry.

When John F. Kennedy established a goal to take a man to the moon, that was a vision. It was like setting a bridge between the present and the future. In a great sense it was also a goal. However, one might distinguish between a vision and a goal by using the example of the man who visualized the game of football. That was a dream of the total picture. The goal of the game, of course, is for each team to take the ball to the opposite end of the field as many times as possible and make points. Therefore, the team with more points wins the game.

Another illustration would be something that happened in the leadership meeting in the southern part of South America. One pastor challenged all of our leaders to have a revival in every church in that area. After much discussion, we decided that his vision was so great that we would have a revival campaign in every church on the continent of South America in the Church of the Nazarene. That vision then became our goal, and we set several steps toward reaching that goal.

Goals should be developed for outreach. New contacts are necessary for reaching goals. As the church reaches out to its community, feet have to be put to those goals so that the Lord can work through people to make it happen. As new contacts are made for the Lord, church members begin

to expect something to happen in their lives and in the lives
of the new contacts. They go in faith, believing that miracles
will be performed.

As vision is received, we need to set goals to accomplish
that vision. Most churches that are not growing have pastors
and congregations who do not expect to grow. Many
churches of 200 members, for example, receive 0-10 new
members in a year. Usually there is something wrong. When
people aim at a goal of 0, they hit it almost every time. That
is not vision for growth. Goals must be realistic, yet stretch-
ing the realm of possibilities. I have seen leaders set goals
that are unreasonable. While I was district superintendent,
one of the pastors set a goal of receiving 100 new members
during the year. That would have been a good goal if it had
been realistic. However, that pastor had never done this kind
of work in all of his ministry. His church was not prepared
for reaching that kind of goal. During the previous year, he
had only received a few members. At the end of that year, he
had only received a few more.

God gave the Christiansted church in the Virgin Islands
a vision to increase their membership. They began to work
to fulfill that vision. God worked among us. The first year
the membership more than doubled with 36 new members
being received, the average attendance for the year also more
than doubled, and the finances more than doubled as well.
The church was extended to three new congregations. The
Lord and His people were building the church.

George Peters considers the following eight elements
necessary for an effective strategy for evangelism.

1. The setting of clearly defined long-range and short-
   range goals
2. Preparation of a realistic timetable to achieve these
   goals
3. The discovery of all possible resources to realize the
   goals

4. The mobilization of personnel and means to actualize the work toward the goals
5. The designing of an appropriate training program of all mobilized personnel to assure the unity, the effectiveness, and the coordination of the work and the accomplishing of the goal
6. The adoption of the most efficient methods to effect the goals
7. The setting up of an appropriate organizational structure in keeping with the dynamic function of the Holy Spirit to carry through the program and consummate the goals
8. The gracious operation of the Holy Spirit in all personnel involved and in all methods and means employed[7]

When we were appointed as pioneer missionaries to open the work for the Church of the Nazarene in the Dominican Republic, I asked the Lord for a vision and a goal. The vision the Lord gave us was to spread scriptural holiness throughout the Dominican Republic. I felt that the Lord gave me a vision and a goal of establishing 50 churches in the first 10 years of the work there. "But Lord," I said, "that rarely has happened in the church in these modern days!" God held me to it. When I shared the vision with my co-worker, Jerry Porter, he said, "Let's do it!" I began asking people to pray that we would reach the goal and fulfill the vision. The Dominicans became involved and caught the vision. God was with us. In 12 years 136 churches had been organized with over 50 missions to be organized. Every pastor and his people can have a vision for growth.

Pastor Harthern admitted that a few years ago he could not have mentally handled a big church. He says that the trouble is that pastors limit God. They learn new methods but would be afraid if the growth came. They could not minister to the people who came and would eventually lose them. Too many pastors are satisfied with a small church and are afraid to continue to grow. The church grows to a certain level and stops because the pastors and laymen do not believe God could do it, or they do not organize for more.

It is God's will that the church grow. Paul in Phil. 4:13 says, "I can do all things through Christ which strengtheneth me." God will give us wisdom and strength and help us to grow the church.

What Do You Think?

1. In addition to the favorable conditions that the pastor can create to have growth and the good methods he can use to reinforce his efforts, what is *essential* for building the church?

2. What is the basis of our authority to go and build the church of God?

3. Why is the church primarily a spiritual center?

4. How can the pastor resolve the following problems in his local church?

      a. How can a church grow if its leaders and members are carnal?

      b. How can a new pastor make the church grow?

      c. How can a pastor grow the church if the members do not want to grow?

5. What is an adequate plan to win the world if 10 denominations planting 100 churches each is not enough?

6. What are the three methods of implementing the plan of "Each One Win One" for your church?

7. What is the difference between the fruits and gifts of the Spirit? What is the purpose of the latter?

8. What is presence evangelism, and where is it necessary to use this method?

9. What is involved in having vision for church growth, and who should have a vision?

2

The Principles—What Others Have Found

Some pastors have never studied church growth principles and are doing an extraordinary job. However, each pastor can learn from the study of church growth principles. Some principles may not work for every pastor, especially if they do not fit the community. You must understand this before beginning to study. But one good idea from someone else put into practice is worthwhile. Many Christian groups around the world have tried and tested the principles of church growth.

Distinctives

Basically, each congregation is distinctive. People choose certain groups for various reasons. One of those reasons is the distinctiveness of their own local church. Denominations will also have distinctives. It seems that different groups grow, not necessarily because of general doctrine, but because of a distinctive doctrine. Groups that are distinctive and emphasize one or two things are the ones that grow the most.

The Nazarenes believe in a second definite work of grace: that God fills the heart of the believer in sanctifying power. That has been the passion of the Church of the Nazarene, their "distinctive."

Whether or not a distinctive is of God or not is probably not a major factor in the area of growth in some groups. The important thing is that distinctives have a special purpose—

to draw people together around a common cause. And, as their people are excited about that purpose, people are willing to give of themselves to build the kingdom of God.

A group should not have a distinctiveness just to be distinctive from another group. A pastor can have a church with a biblical purpose and the power of God working and living in the lives of the people. This distinctiveness needs to be developed as an asset of growth and needs to be kept in front of the people constantly.

Many groups have built their whole church by preaching the standards of the church. Standards are an important aspect of the church, to be sure, but more important is the doctrine of the church. Major on the majors, and minor on the minors. Doctrine is definitely a major part of the church; standards are but a minor part. Place the emphasis on doctrine, not on standards.

Standards, however, have their place in the church. Dean M. Kelly tries to answer why conservative churches are growing. He says,

> Those who are serious about their faith:
> 1. Do not confuse it with other beliefs, loyalties, practices or mingle them together indiscriminately, or pretend they are alike, of equal merit, or mutually compatible if they are not.
> 2. Make high demands of those admitted to the organization that bears the faith, and do not include or allow to continue within it those who are not fully committed to it.
> 3. Do not consent to encourage, or indulge any violations of its standards of belief or behavior by its professed adherents.
> 4. Do not keep silent about it, apologize for it, or let it be treated as though it made no difference, or should make no difference, in their behavior or in their relationships with others.[1]

Many times people have told me that they want to be a part of a church that has standards. "Liberalizing standards and requirements for church membership has not produced any phenomenal church growth. The churches in which members can believe and act in any way and still be members of the church in good standing are having little or no growth."[2]

When the church's goal is self-preservation (institutionalism), it tries to control by giving tighter supervision and limiting the spontaneity and involvement of its people. As an institution it will eventually begin to taper off and decrease in membership.

The church must have a good reputation in the community. It must have a symbolic identity. The community must see that the church is ready and willing to do something for God.

It is as a dynamic movement that the church grows. A movement is usually a growing force, alive and exciting. Something is happening, and there is a purpose for existing. If the church is to grow, the pastor develops an image of a movement. A movement will build strong priorities into its people and call them to loyalty and sacrifice of themselves, their finances, and their time in order to build the kingdom of God. There will be constant recruitment by all of the people, and the constant training of new leaders and new workers is important. A movement is a mighty force for God.

Groups

Several factors concerning the groups of the church create favorable conditions for growth. The many potential groups in the local church must be developed and their potential tapped. Groups can be exciting tools to help the church move forward and play an important role in creating the conditions for church growth.

Small churches may be comprised of one primary group in their congregations. It is usually a tightly woven group composed of family and friends. This limits growth. The small church can only minister to the type of people that fit into that group. Sometimes a small church is unwilling to accept someone outside of their group. They run people away from the church before accepting a stranger, especially if he is different from the group. A story of a layman from the Central District in Argentina illustrates this fact. He went to the church several times, called the pastor several times, but finally gave up. He then proceeded to visit other churches, but he did not feel comfortable in any of them. Finally after the church had changed pastors, he made one more try, which turned out to be successful with the new pastor. The new pastor led him to receive Christ and then brought him into the fellowship of the church. He is now a very successful layman and important member of that church.

The small church concept is interested in maintaining unity and keeping its family of believers together. It wants everyone to be the same. The single group of a small church has to be broken down into a variety of small groups in order to promote growth.

A large church, on the other hand, has many small groups, almost like several small churches within one large church. People find their own group for fellowship, which becomes their church family. At the same time they are involved in the total program of the church, which helps involve them in other groups as well.

For a small church to grow, groups need to be developed. These can be at the level of the Sunday School classes, interest groups, geographical cells, and prayer groups. Some of the divisions will come naturally. This can be done as the pastor trains the people to reach out to the community and then to create the atmosphere that will make new people feel welcome in the church.

One important factor of growth in the local church is that new groups tend to grow faster than old groups. If the church is not starting new groups, then growth will tend to slow.

New cells and new people expand the growing edge of every church. These new groups must have leadership so that creating a new group provides the opportunity to involve new leaders and new officers for the group. Their goal is to reach out and bring others into their fellowship.

For many years the Sunday School has had the concept of divide and grow. If a class runs 20, then division into two groups helps growth. Usually both groups will soon be running 20 in attendance. Therefore, if we continue to divide the church into different leadership groups, the church will tend to grow as each individual group grows.

We have the same situation on the district level. If the district leader wants to pastor all of the churches, then he will probably have only one church. However, if the district leader takes 20 men and puts them in 20 different locations, he can help them develop their congregations. In a short time he will be pastoring via the pastors to 20 different groups. This mirrors the plan for growth through groups in the local church. The pastor will be the pastor of 20 groups only if he has 20 lay leaders working with him. His goal is to help them launch 20 different groups in the local church. As each group grows, the church grows. That is certainly much faster than having just one group growing in the local church.

Of the three basic types of groups in the church, the first is nurture groups. Methodism started in nurture groups—class meetings. These groups were one key to their growth. Nurture groups may be neighborhood Bible studies or prayer meetings. Every church needs nurture groups. They meet together for encouragement and spiritual growth.

The second group is the outreach group. Certainly the Sunday School class with outreach as one of its emphases falls into this category. Discipling groups, soul-winning groups, visitation groups, and home Bible study groups are all outreach groups. Their nature is to evangelize.

A third type of group is the service group. Churches can have different kinds of service groups such as the choir, ushers, the church board, youth groups, as well as fellowship and ministry groups. If the church does not develop these and other service groups, then leadership and growth will be limited.

Paul Orjala says, "There are two kinds of *outreach groups* that every church needs: (1) Those that serve as *points of contact* for evangelism; (2) Those that can serve as *points of entry* for getting new people into the church. Some can serve *both purposes.*"[3]

It is common knowledge that the numbers increase much faster with multiplication than with addition. The multiplication principle is valuable in church growth as well. If the pastor wins one person every week to Jesus Christ, and to the church, that certainly does add. That would be 52 new converts every year in the church. However, if the pastor teaches 20 laymen to win one new person every week, then that would be 1,040 souls won in a year—plus the pastor's 52!

Not only are individuals won, but groups of people can be won, multiplying the church's growth at a much faster rate. Often it may be just as easy to win an entire family instead of just the mother or one of the children. In cultures that are group-oriented and family-oriented, the gospel can be presented to groups of people. A collective decision to accept Jesus as Lord is done just as easily as individually. It seems that the apostle Paul used the people movement—

members of a close-knit group seeking to persuade their loved ones to believe on the Lord Jesus Christ and be saved. In Acts 16:14-15, we see this in the story of Lydia. Also, in the case of the jailer later in the same chapter, the decision was made by the whole family to follow Christ. "Often they will defer their own decision in order to be baptized together. A husband waits six months for an unbelieving wife."[4] While this pattern does not mean group conversion, it does mean that individually they will make a decision together to turn their lives over to Jesus Christ.

Pastor and People

What is the pastor's relation to these principles of church growth? There is no more important question than this for the pastor who desires that his church grow. He must decide how many of the church growth principles he is going to learn and put into practice. Some may say, "It is not worth it." Others do not want to put the time and effort into it. However, if he wants to be God's man to help God's Church grow, then he needs to develop some church growth principles. Here are three growth principles for the pastor of a soul-winning church.

A pastor must first be willing to pay the price in hard work for his church to grow. If a church is growing, then it has a hardworking pastor. There is no "40-hour workweek" in the life of the pastor. He will need to work 60 and 80 hours a week in order to prepare his messages, do visitation, and minister to the needs of the congregation. It is not the busy work that will build the church, but work that has been prioritized to achieve the most results. There will be little time left for his personal pleasures. A growing church may be enjoyable to the pastor, but it is not easy.

The pastor has to be willing to pay the price to have church members with whom he cannot be personally involved. After a church gets very large, a pastor can deal with his people only so often. His pastoral visits to the same people will be less frequent because there are more who need his care and support. Therefore, he is going to have to delegate pastoral responsibility to different ones in the congregation. He will have to ask others to help with the hospital, shut-in, and even new contact visitation. He will need to share leadership as well. The sharing of leadership might be on the staff level or the lay level. Thus he will discover that he is not personally involved with all of his people. Not only does the pastor have to be willing to pay the price for growth, but the laity of a growing church must be willing not to have the minister personally come to their home every few days or few weeks. Their goal should be to be involved in ministry as well, not to wait on the pastor, but to become involved in reaching new people.

The people must be willing to follow church growth leadership. One of the reasons some churches do not grow is because they are not following their leader. This will require a new mentality for some.

An important characteristic of a growing congregation is that it must be willing to pay the bills. It costs money to build and expand the church. It costs money for salaries, equipment, materials, and supplies. The congregation must be willing to tithe and give offerings in order to make it happen. Of course the pastor sets the example in stewardship.

A significant characteristic of a growing congregation is that it is willing to adjust and readjust the fellowship patterns. Christian fellowship is essential for church growth. The congregation must be willing to include strangers in its groups. People will feel welcome and easily become a part of a group.

A repeated problem for most churches is the length of the pastorates. Small churches change their pastor frequently. From one to two years he is learning how his people think and is developing them. Usually after about two years he begins his ministry to the community. Actually a pastor needs about four years to have any in-depth effect on a community. Anything less than four or five years is considered a short pastorate. When a church is growing, one of the best ways to hinder that growth is to change its pastor. "In the churches with the 10 largest Sunday schools in America, Elmer Towns discovered a few years ago that the average length of pastorate was 22 years and one month."[5]

Pastor Don Wellman says that evidently God does not want large churches. The average length of the pastorate in the United States in the Church of the Nazarene is three years and two months. Wellman says that every one of those pastors who has moved after a short time states that God told them to move. "Since you cannot build a large church in so short a time, evidently God does not want large churches." That may be a little sarcastic; however, it does reveal to us some of our own mentality in staying with the job and building a great church.

Peter Wagner writes about this type of problem, "Many churches don't grow because a strong-minded group of lay leaders has gained control of them and they have long since decided not to surrender their leadership to any pastor. Their usual tactic for preserving that control is to change pastors every two to five years. This is highly effective in prohibiting any pastor from usurping their leadership power. It is equally effective in keeping a lid on the growth of the church."[6]

Four ground rules for church growth apply to the pastor and the local church. First, the pastor should not try to copy the style, goals, and plans for growth of another pastor. He should make his own plans, seek his own goals, develop his own strategy, and create a successful style for ministry. If he can copy a good idea from another pastor, he may borrow the concept and consolidate it with his plan and make it his own. He must not be under bondage to be like someone else.

Second, there may have to be a big push to make the church begin to grow. For example, it takes more power to get a car moving from a complete stop than it does to keep the car moving. Getting the church into a moving pattern for growth after it has been at a standstill for some time may take a major power. However, after the church is moving, increased activity does not necessarily give growth. Adding to the activity level may only add to frustration. Priorities must be set to assure the activities are producing growth.

Third, praying and believing will not produce shortcuts to church growth. If the church prays all day and all night for weeks and believes that God is going to send many people into the church, that will not necessarily produce church growth. Church growth takes putting feet to those prayers. God is going to have to deal with the laymen and the pastor about their commitment and involvement. They both must be willing to be used as instruments to produce church growth as God works through them.

Fourth, remember that the primary object is the spiritual growth of many people, not just great numbers of people. Numbers do not automatically mean church growth. However, when the people are present, they can be helped spiritually. The appropriate emphasis is on furthering spiritual growth as well as increasing the size of the congregation.

Just as there must be a good foundation in order to have a good, strong building, the same is true for Christian believers. They must be well-grounded in the Word of God and strong in their own spiritual lives. Then they are able to reach out to the lost to help the church grow.

Pastor Harthern shares these seven spiritual principles that are needed for church growth:

1. The Lord, not the pastor, must build the church.
2. What is born of the Spirit is Spirit, but what is born of the flesh is flesh. God's answer to the flesh is crucifixion. If the pastor has to push and push to keep a program alive, Pastor Harthern believes he should let it die. Period.
3. People come where they get fed. It's like a restaurant. People will drive past many eating establishments to find the one where the atmosphere is right and the food is good.
4. Pastors should quit praying, "God, bless what I'm doing." Instead, they should pray, "God, help me to do what You are blessing."
5. Develop your faith. "You can have what you believe for," Pastor Harthern preaches. "If you don't believe God to do anything in your church, He won't."
6. Church growth comes from a willingness to rely totally on the Holy Spirit, Pastor Harthern teaches. Sometimes this is difficult, especially if it means creating new wineskins to hold the "new wine" of the Holy Spirit.
7. Objectives are important. Pastor Harthern's primary objective is training leaders. He tries to impart his own exciting, dynamic faith that God can do the impossible.[7]

Ralph Winter suggests four areas of growth that may be found in the local church.

1. *Internal* growth is the development of qualitative growth within the church, sometimes referred to as *nurture.* This involves doctrinal teaching and formation of ethical and spiritual patterns of life, and is the starting point for all other forms of church growth. Without internal growth, the church cannot be the Church.

2. *Expansion* growth is the numerical growth of the local church as new converts are won and incorporated into the church. This involves winning your own kind of people from the surrounding unchristian society.

3. *Extension* growth refers to the *planting of new churches* in the same society as the original churches.

4. *Bridging* growth is characterized by the planting of churches across a cultural barrier. This is typical missionary work, whether home missions among people of a contrasting culture, or world missions abroad. The name refers to "bridging" across cultures.[8]

The principles of church growth are a means to the end, not an end in themselves. Their implementation will change with individual situations. The pastor will profit by knowing as many principles as possible and choosing the ones that fit the local setting. God's purpose is to make disciples; therefore we must find the most effective ways to have the greatest success possible.

What Do You Think?

1. Why is it important for a Christian group to have distinctives? What is the distinctive of the Church of the Nazarene?

2. What is a dynamic movement, and how does it help church growth?

3. What church growth problem does the small church have, and how can it be resolved?

4. Explain the principle of multiplication in relation to church growth.

5. What does it mean that the pastor must "pay the price" for his church to grow?

6. How much time is needed for a pastor to learn to know his congregation? How can the departure of a pastor affect the growth of the local church?

7. Mention and explain the four rules for growth that apply to the pastor and the local church.

8. Why does a great number of people not necessarily mean church growth?

3

The Conditions

Planning

Church growth is directly proportional to favorable conditions at the local level. One key to revival is atmosphere. The pastor is always the key in setting the pace and creating the right conditions for the total church. He can teach the people and help them understand what their role is in creating those conditions. He can plan ways to develop the right circumstances that will promote growth.

If a local church is to see results, it must prepare. Preparation means prework and planning to organize the local church in such a way that it can take advantage of growth conditions. Planning is essential for every church. Although loose organization is sufficient in some situations, there must be organization, and that takes preplanning. Organization prepares the people for church growth conditions. Without organization and preplanning, the local church has no direction. It is like taking a vacation trip with no destination. The pastor should plan as if everything depends upon his planning, but he should be willing to change those plans as the Holy Spirit directs. He also prepares the people for various programs of the church. Organization is the skeleton that provides a framework for the church to mobilize for growth.

Programs are to be developed in each church that will fit every age-group. There should be programs for the whole church. The purpose of programs for the growing church is not just to make people busy but to minister and reach out to the unsaved. While programs have a lot to do with creating favorable conditions for church growth, they are not in themselves ends. Laypeople must be willing to give of themselves and their time to carry on those programs, for the pastor cannot bear the burden of running all the programs himself. Programs provide opportunities for ministry for laymen.

The pastor can oversee the laymen as they carry on the ministry of the programs. He is not afraid to try new programs. He might try a new program of visitation with one-to-one soul winning, Caravans and quizzing for the youth, and install the Cradle Roll program for winning new families. In South America we are using a program "Each One Win One." Each church member is challenged to win one person to Christ during the year, disciple him, and guide him into church membership. The membership has grown from 16,000 to 49,000 in five years. This program can be used in small and large churches. If a program does not work, then it has to be changed. Something else must be tried. The creative pastor finds the ones that work in his local church.

Prayer and Bible Study

Every church, if it is going to be a spiritual church, needs groups of people praying for the growth of the local church and the movement of the Holy Spirit in the church services. Prayer prepares the hearts of the people to receive the message.

Prayer may be on the individual or group level. A group of at least two or three people who gather together in the local church is a prayer cell. Their concern is with the on-going and growing factor of the church. These groups expect something to happen in a service or in a series of services. Their attitude of expectancy about the church may be the difference between a dead or alive church.

Mike Johnson, the pastor of a large church in the

United States, said, "The first key to church growth is prayer. We have an every Saturday night prayer group of 400 people who come to seek God. Another key is work. Nothing works by itself. I tell the people to put legs on their prayers."[1]

Johnson's church jumped to an average of over 2,100 people in attendance in only nine years. He built his church on prayer and work. At first few attended the prayer meetings, but he continued them in spite of the poor attendance. He believed that prayer changes things, and it did. His church grew. Prayer and work go together. When the people are praying, they begin to work, and things begin to happen. There will be more love among the brethren, and there will be more concern for the unsaved. Also, they will consecrate everything to God, tithing their resources, time, and talents. Prayer and growth will revitalize the spiritual condition of the local church.

Bible study is another important adventure that produces good conditions for church growth. Bible study can be programmed in many different ways and can include the whole church. Group studies are effective for studying God's Word and for getting the people into that good habit. Through the Word of God people's hearts come alive, and they become more receptive to the Spirit speaking through His Word. Bible study challenges the people, which encourages them to go on and do greater things for the building of the kingdom of God.

In addition to studying the Bible, another important step is to involve people in leading Bible studies. The pastor can organize several different Bible studies throughout the church in the homes of the people. This takes the study of the Word to where the people live, and they can in turn involve their neighbors. Many times new people will become hungry to accept Jesus Christ as their Lord through Bible studies.

Laymen who will be leading Bible studies may need special training. They should learn how to use study aids such as commentaries, and they will need help learning what and how to study. A Bible study group is a vital extension and feeder of the local church. Bible studies create a tremendous condition for helping the church grow!

This is also true in Bible teaching in the Sunday School classes. Several church growth experts have confirmed this concept. "The Sunday schools which have experienced continual growth during the seventies have been those which have been built upon a systematic, comprehensive teaching of Scripture and doctrine. It is possible for a Sunday School to mushroom overnight. But many of those that did not have quality teaching soon topped out. Some reversed the trend. The Sunday School of the future should not have to sacrifice growth for Bible teaching; both can operate together."[2]

Expectation

For church growth to occur, people have to expect something to happen in their church. When they come to church and feel an excitement about the outcome of the service, they will carry that excitement to their friends and neighbors. They will tell people what God is doing. People talk about their relationship to Christ and to the church. The carnal church talks only about itself. The growing church talks about Jesus Christ and the excitement taking place within the services. The power of Jesus is manifest.

There are probably some circumstances in the community the church can take advantage of. People are more receptive under certain conditions. When people have taken new jobs and moved into new communities, they are more willing to break traditional and religious background ties. When there are family crises such as deaths, sickness, and loss of employment, people are more willing to turn to God.

After we had been in the Dominican Republic for a couple of years, and the church was growing at a rapid rate, other denominations began to ask: "If your church can grow, why can't our church grow?" They began to look around for reasons. They found we were preaching the message of holiness and trusting the Holy Spirit to help us reach the lost. They found we were trusting new converts and training them on the job to be pastors. They found that church growth was spontaneous as established congregations, though new, were planning and starting new churches without tight control from the denominational leaders. They found that we were trusting new converts to become active church members, and we were not requiring them to wait during a long probation period. As they began to use some of these ideas, they began to grow as well as start new churches. Their enthusiasm ignited a new spark.

In his class Paul Orjala discusses three factors that help people respond to the gospel of Christ.

The *first* is that people are responsive when we meet their perceived needs. Most of the time, a person's decision is contingent upon feeling that his needs have been met. A pastor is successful as he helps people move closer to having faith in Jesus Christ. The pastor can find examples of this right in his community. Someone in his community has all of the material needs that he desires. He may have a background in a religion. However, he does not go to church because he has no desire to do so.

The *second* factor is to use the approach that suits their motivation and their value system. Fit the approach to the person. Presenting the gospel to a Roman Catholic would be entirely different than presenting the gospel to someone who has no religious background. One needs to consider the church background, the environmental background, and the secular world of the person he is trying to win.

The *third* factor is that if the *right* person shares the gospel with another, he is more likely to respond positively. By that we mean someone that the individual trusts. The soul winner wins the person to himself before he can win him to Jesus Christ. Most people who are won to Christianity today are friends of the one who introduced him to Jesus. This is one reason the universal witness is so important. All have friends. Those friends can be introduced to Jesus. What about the Christians who have all of their friends in the church? If they do not have friends who are not Christians, there are acquaintances that could be developed into friendships such as classmates, work colleagues, and public service workers. Perhaps the church can help redirect priorities in outreach ministries for the members.

Newness and Crises

There are other factors in the community that will help church growth. One is industrialization, which in itself may not bring people to church but does, however, bring them to your community. Their moving breaks ties with their old establishment, making them more open to the gospel. They do not feel as obligated to maintain the family religious practices when they move some distance from the home area.

Beginning a new church in an old community where most families have lived for years is difficult. Churches started on the edge of the city and in transient areas tend to grow better. Newcomers living in an area open it up to church planting. A person coming to a new community is a person removed from his past. He has left his old friends. Usually he has left his church. His social contacts are left behind too. He is looking for new friends, new contacts, and an opportunity to establish his family in the new community. He is probably more open to the gospel after having moved from one community to another than at any other time.

With this advantage of receptivity, the pastor needs to be there when the new person arrives, or just a few days later.

In some communities, the Chamber of Commerce is glad to provide names and addresses of people moving to the community. Laymen in the church can be constantly on the lookout for signs of people moving into their neighborhoods, and they then are ready to alert the pastor. He in turn needs to assign one of his laymen to make contact with the new neighbor and become his friend. Said layman should invite the neighbor to church as well as take the church to his home. The secret is to include him in the group. Then the gospel can be presented after he is hungry and searching for something new in his life.

The youth of almost every country are open to the gospel. If the major emphasis of the church's work is with children, the church will take 15 years to grow up. If the church works primarily with adults, they are not among the most receptive. They are usually satisfied with the old establishment. Young people, however, are often dissatisfied and looking for meaning in life. They are searching for a better way than their fathers had. Tomorrow's youth will be the adult church.

The time in a person's life when he is most receptive to receive ministry is when he is in crisis. Usually a person will respond to that which will help him in his need. This is one of the purposes of the church. The Christian has Christ to help in the time of need. The sinner has no one to turn to. Since crises occur in almost everyone's life, if the church is there at that point of time in that person's life, then it can minister to him, bringing him to Jesus.

Crisis comes when there is a threat to the future of the person. There are several types of crises. Special crisis times would be the death of a family member or friend, job loss or other significant losses, and sickness. Times of sickness, especially serious illnesses, find people more open to the gospel. This is an open door for the church to minister to hurting people. Stay alert for opportunities to minister to those in crisis.

A couple experienced the suicide of their son. Two years later in the fall a teenage girl in their small community took her life. The couple visited the family each week. They just went to the door and got in to *share their sorrow!* Easter Sunday the new family attended church for the first time.

Political change can create a crisis sufficient to bring people to the understanding that they are not self-sufficient. People are more open during civil unrest. A high or increased crime rate in the community and social changes foster openness to the gospel.

Jesus spoke to those with felt needs when He said, "Come unto me, all ye that labour and are heavy laden, and I will give you rest" (Matt. 11:28). The church concentrates on the responsive. While they will not ignore the resistant, the church will put its emphasis on winning the receptive. Someday the resistant may be responsive; then the church will be called on to help because they know the church is their friend. The gospel should be presented to the whole family while they are receptive.

"They are most often responsive when others are moving toward the gospel. Don't be satisfied with just one person—try for the whole family, the whole group. Don't lose time; press the issue immediately. Train new Christians right away to win their families and friends."[3]

Often a congregation and their pastor will say, "When we have a church building, then we can grow." This statement is not valid. A building usually does help growth; but if a congregation is not growing, to blame it on the building or the lack of a building is not the answer. When the building is new, some members will be excited; but after its newness is gone, people will slump back into their former patterns. A building can be a tremendous asset, but a building is not an automatic answer for growth.

The kingdom of God is not a building. The location of the church is in every believer. The building is only a congregating place. When the pastor dismisses a church service, the church disburses into the community. "Know ye not that ye are the temple of God, and that the spirit of God dwelleth in you?" (1 Cor. 3:16).

People share with others that Jesus is in their lives. The building will not talk, except in its appearance, but the people will share because of the beauty of Christ in them. God wants to dwell continually among the people. "I will live in them and move among them, and I will be their God, and they shall be my people" (2 Cor. 6:16, RSV).

The Bible teaches that the Christian is the temple of the Lord. Luke states in Acts 17:24, "He . . . dwelleth not in temples made with hands." Christ wants to abide in the believer. Buildings are instruments to use for the glory of God and to congregate the people. The Early Church grew, even though the Christians had no church buildings of their own. In some cases they used temples or synagogues. Most of their churches were in their houses. "Archaeologists report no findings of church buildings constructed from the birth of Christ until after A.D. 150."[4] They preached wherever there were people.

In the New Testament they seemed to understand that house churches would help them to get out among their people. That concept can be used today. House churches can be extensions of the local church. Every house church or extension of the local church exposes the church to a new section of society in that community. More people have a closer contact with the church.

A church building should be adequate for evangelism, worship, and education. Its construction should correspond with the surrounding community to be acceptable to the people of the community. The building should be built to appear inviting to the community, yet it need not be elaborate. Its appearance is how the community sees the body of Christ.

The maintenance of the building is important. Neglecting the facility is a harmful witness for the church. Keep the church clean and neat in appearance outside as well as inside. Many members and friends of the church have abilities and skills that they can use to keep the building in good repair and clean. Many times church people get so accustomed to seeing the church "the way it is" that they fail to see it as a visitor would see it. An uninviting, dirty, or junk-filled building may turn someone away from Jesus.

While the building has its role to play, church growth conditions are affected directly by the type of church services that are celebrated in that building. The pastor should not try to make the services something the people of the community are not. Whatever order the service takes, the focal point should be the Word of God. Services should be varied, with the power of the Holy Spirit moving the people. The variety from service to service should not be so much that people are confused when they attend the services.

In Latin America the pastor often lets someone else run the preliminary service. While this is permissible, the pastor needs to be the one who sets the direction and the climate of the service. He is the motivator of the people. He knows the direction in which the church needs to go. The pastor needs to put people to work in the service and control the direction of that service. Everything in the service should be done with a purpose: to draw people to Jesus. The most effective service for bringing people to a decision is an evangelistic service where people are presented the gospel and brought face-to-face with their spiritual needs.

Atmosphere

Probably more important than what is said during the

service is its atmosphere. The atmosphere should be joyful, Spirit-filled, and speak to people, motivating them to want to be a part of that congregation and a part of Christ. That atmosphere also blesses mature Christians, motivating them to live deeper Christian lives and to share their lives with others. Since people are naturally emotional, religion must appeal not only to the intellect but also to the emotions.

The type of service determines how appealing the church will be. Having emotional services is important with good teaching from the Word of God. The guidance of the Holy Spirit in the church provides the balance. Growing churches in Latin American countries may have hand clapping while they sing lively choruses, helping to make an emotional service. Many of those churches have found the right balance of emotion. They have the fire of the Holy Spirit, but they do not have the wildfire that leads to confusion. Their enthusiasm for the Lord shows. People come to their churches to see what is happening because the members are enthusiastic and their lives are being changed.

The first visible evidence of enthusiasm is in the singing—a very important part of worship. Some like music that is more emotional, while others prefer a more dignified variety. The pastor can help the church decide on a balance of music that will create the right condition for the Holy Spirit to speak to first-time visitors and mature Christians alike.

Creating a church choir can be one of the greatest assets to church music your church can have. Special singing along with good congregational singing that is alive and speaks to people is important. Use evangelistic songs. Developing a good music program will take work and planning, but it is worth it. Most growing churches around the world have a musical program. This can also happen in small, growing churches. I remember the church where I was converted. They had 50-60 people in attendance each Sunday morning.

The church was growing and developing new pastors constantly. The people did not have the great talent that you find in many churches; however, the people were excited about participating and glorifying God. I drove 50 miles one way just to attend that small church because of the atmosphere and program that they had.

All of the studying and learning and planning for growing the church are great assets. Planning is important, but plans are not enough. Emotion is not enough. Great music and choirs are not enough. The right order of service is not enough. Only the Holy Spirit is enough. The Spirit must lead the pastor and the church.

I have been in churches that have so much enthusiasm and emotion that they neglect the leadership of the Holy Spirit. Other churches follow the order of service so closely that the Lord could not possibly break in on them. There is a balance, and the pastor's task is to find that balance as he leads the church. An inviting pulpit encourages people to attend the church. Most great churches are pastored by pulpiteers. However, if the pastor is not a super preacher, that does not mean that the church cannot grow. He can find the balance of making the messages speak to the needs of the people. They will be able to invite their friends and be proud of the pastor.

People want an experience that is real. Excessive emotionalism is detrimental to the church and will drive visitors away. The church should be real and genuine as it carries out its message.

Likewise tradition can be a barrier to church growth. Churches that hold on to tradition substitute it for meeting the real needs of the church and the community. If a program has no real purpose, the church should not continue it for the sake of tradition. The ultimate goal and rationale for providing programs and activities at all should be for making disciples and winning people to Christ.

A similar barrier is the failure of a church to want to learn church growth principles and put them into practice. The church is satisfied with its present growth. However, if the pastor is to lead the church to growth, he has to face those problems and break down those barriers.

First, he should examine your church to find out what kinds of barriers are hindering church growth. In a positive way, seek to remove those barriers one by one. I would suggest using the Word of God to show that the church can grow. Other ways would be to study what some have done in breaking down those barriers in their churches. Seek help from successful pastors who may have had some of the same experiences you are having.

A perpetual problem with most churches is that they are bringing people in the front door while others are leaving through the back door just as quickly. Many churches have a 50 percent loss or turnover in the period of a decade. Between 1972 and 1978 the Church of the Nazarene had a 46 percent turnover. In one of his seminary classes, Paul Orjala gave five reasons for this loss or turnover: *(a)* spiritual regression; *(b)* inadequate follow-up; *(c)* failure of involvement; *(d)* failure in fellowship; *(e)* social-economic mismatch.

Another aspect of growth and loss is that every church grows biologically. As new children are born to the families of the church, the pastor needs to win those children intentionally, for God has no grandchildren. Their commitment to Jesus Christ must be personal, too.

The other side of this is loss by death. Loss of membership by death will occur in every church at some time. People will move away, also, leaving a loss of membership. This kind of loss cannot be controlled.

There are ways for the church to keep its members. Somehow the church has to stop the unnecessary flow of people leaving the church before lasting church growth can be realized. Good fellowship can be one way to involve new people immediately. Actually, follow-up can be accomplished by establishing a conservation program in the church to keep as many people as possible. Follow-up includes frequent contact with the new people. Keeping the members of the church in harmony and fellowship will maintain their loyalty to the local church.

A discipling program also keeps people from leaving the church. In the Great Commission of Matthew 28 Jesus says to go into all the world and make disciples. Making disciples means bringing unbelievers into the Body of Christ in such a way that they will make a decision, realize the presence of the resurrected Christ, and commit to personal involvement. Then, as disciples, they are trained for witnessing, which helps establish them. The primary task of evangelism is making disciples. When a person is established in his faith in Jesus Christ and established in the local church as a working, witnessing member, he will be less likely to leave that fellowship. Virgil Gerber gives three things that the Scriptures made evident concerning making disciples.

1. Evangelism and discipling in the New Testament are inseparably linked together.
2. Evangelism and discipling in the New Testament focus on the church.
3. Evangelism and discipling in the New Testament are not complete until: *(a)* converts are incorporated into churches, *(b)* churches have been firmly planted and have taken root in every part of the world.[5]

Another way to grow is to receive new members. Without new members, the church becomes static and eventually lifeless. It loses its purpose. The will of God is for every church to grow. That means bringing new persons into the fellowship of the church. Goals are to be set and plans made for receiving members every month, with a total goal of new members for the year. Goals should be reasonable and reachable, yet challenging. Probably as a guideline, 15-20 percent increase each year in membership would be a gratifying goal. Many try to increase by a greater percentage.

The pastor incorporates the new members into the Body of Christ by baptism and reception as church members. He helps to establish them in Christian behavior. As the necessary growth and maturity occur, tithing and bonding to the fellowship will be fulfilled. The pastor helps them to recognize their spiritual gifts and trains them for witness and the ministry.

Responsiveness and resistance are two important factors to recognize in church growth. People can only be won when they are responsive. The receptivity of a person changes according to events, cultures, and happenings in their lives. As the pastor sows the seed and waters, the resistance to the gospel is broken down. The pastor needs to take advantage of every responsive situation.

Paul Orjala explains why people are resistant. He believes the first reason is that they may have an ignorance of the gospel. The problem of many is that they lack information. They have not had the contact. They misunderstand what the gospel of Jesus Christ is all about. Therefore, there may be a tremendous ignorance of the gospel in the locality of the church.

The second reason is that people feel self-sufficient. They have no sense of need. Maybe they are affluent and have been successful. Many times their religion or materialism is satisfying at least their felt needs. Why should they accept the gospel when everything else is going fine?

The third reason is neglect by the church. In the shadow of every church are people who are searching for something to satisfy, but often the church inadvertently neglects people, and they feel unwanted. Their low self-esteem and few Christian acquaintances render them resistant because of the church's neglect. They remain unreached.

The fourth reason is that many people have spiritual vacuums. They will not have a sense of guilt. Many have not experienced God's presence or His power. Certainly there are many in this world who are in religious bondage. They live in fear. There is substitution of other things for religion. Until a spiritual vacuum is recognized as a need, people tend to be resistant to the gospel. This actually occurred in Acts 2:43.

The church will not grow if we are not alert to the situations around us. The secular business world is always aware of the marketing possibilities. They spend millions of dollars making sure their product will be marketable. How much more should we investigate all possibilities for winning the lost.

In Luke 15 we find three parables. There was a different method used in each case of recovering the lost sheep, the lost coin, and the prodigal son. Immediately following these parables, we have the story of the unjust steward. "And the lord commended the unjust steward, because he had done wisely" (Luke 16:8). The Lord wants us to be wise in everything that we do and do our best to reach the lost for Him.

What Do You Think?

1. Why is planning important for church growth?

2. What is the purpose of programs in the local church?

3. Why is prayer necessary for church growth, and with what should it be combined?

4. What is the place of Bible studies in the local church and in the growth of the church? Who should direct the Bible studies, and why?

5. What is the place of the Sunday School in church growth?

6. What are the conditions of receptiveness in the community that the local church ought to take advantage of?

7. Explain the factors that help people respond to the gospel of Christ. Which social groups are most receptive? What age is most receptive to the gospel?

8. In what sense are believers the temple of God? Why is this concept important for church growth?

9. Why should the pastor take the lead in the order and celebration of church services? In what way does a service whose purpose is to lead others to Christ promote church growth?

10. What is essential for church growth? Why will a church with adequate plans and programs fail if the Holy Spirit is not present?

4

The Pastor

The Pastor as Preacher

The apostle Paul was a man who dedicated his life to the preaching of the gospel. He had a reason. As he writes in 1 Cor. 9:16, the reader can see his heartbeat. He declares that he has to preach the gospel. The pastor will feel that way. He will not be content to sit back and listen to someone else preach all of the time, for there is always that urgency to proclaim the message of Christ from the pulpit, even though the Lord may change the types of ministries that he will do.

It is often difficult to understand the purpose of preaching. It seems rather trite for one to stand before a congregation and raise his voice as he delivers a message from the Lord. However, that is God's chosen method of public proclamation, mystical in the sense that it is more than just a man speaking, it is God taking His message to individuals. God has ordained "by the foolishness of preaching to save them that believe" (1 Cor. 1:21). He has called ministers to be obedient servants in that proclamation of the gospel.

Biblical preaching is best for delivering the message of the Lord. At times it is easier to take a text and preach one's own ideas, but such preaching lacks the depth necessary for understanding and growth. Biblical preaching involves expositional-type messages. It is not what an individual says but what God says through that person. An expositional sermon is prepared by exegetical study of the Word. It will require more study and preparation but is far more rewarding. It lives! People can remember the message and make the

55

truths apply to their lives. It will mold them into the shape that God wants to form them. Expositional sermons are most effective in helping Christians grow.

Not only does this type of preaching offer practical, Bible-based help while it matures believers in their walk with God, but the messenger can preach without fear. Occasionally people will feel that they are being preached at. They become angry. However, if the message comes directly from the Bible, personalities and preachers are removed from the message. God speaks directly to the receiver.

In addition to exegetical content, an evangelistic preaching style can be used by all who proclaim the Word. While there are appropriate styles for different occasions, it is important to use the evangelistic style to obtain the results of souls being saved and sanctified. Many good pastors who are quiet by nature have learned to use an evangelistic style in preference to a teaching style in their preaching.

An evangelistic style means delivering the message with the purpose of convincing the congregation to be obedient to God's message. Although the voice may be soft at times, it should be firm and pleasant. The minister is obligated to preach with power. That power is twofold: human and divine. Deliver the message with as much human power as possible. Use force, emphasize points with gestures, raise and lower the voice, and speak with a sense of urgency. The power of God is manifest through the style and content of the message.

Evangelistic preaching releases the power of the gospel of Christ. The Lord will call people from sin to holiness. The Holy Spirit will convict and convince of sins. Evangelistic preaching will draw believers into a deeper and closer relationship with Christ, and the Lord will call workers to the harvest.

Preparation for evangelistic, exegetical preaching is

very important. Plan to spend several blocks of time each week in preparation for God's messages. The continual preparation is very important. The effective preacher collects thoughts months in advance as seed thoughts for future sermons. He lives in the Word. The Word must come alive through him to his people.

Pray until you can preach with brokenness. Prayer is so necessary that it cannot be overemphasized. Your life should be filled with the Holy Spirit so that you can be the best vessel possible. Preaching is serious, and if you enter the pulpit without adequate prayer, someone will pay the costly price.

One Sunday night I was preaching in a new church in Santo Domingo, Dominican Republic. I had prepared for the sermon through study and prayer. While I was preaching, the Lord came in a special way, and in brokenness I cried. When the altar call was given, Renne, a young combo singer, stepped out and accepted Christ as his Savior. Later he testified and said, "I don't remember anything that Bro. Bustle said; but when he cried, I was impressed that if the message meant so much to him, I needed that experience." Renne grew rapidly in the faith and pastored several strong churches in the Dominican Republic and is now serving as a district superintendent there.

There is no substitute for the unction of the Holy Spirit. It keeps the message from being hollow. It fills the air with expectancy. When the minister preaches with unction, preparation and delivery are at their best, and the Holy Spirit fills the gap between the man and God's message. If a minister has never preached with the unction of the Holy Spirit, he has not seen his greatest potential. Unction is the special help given by the Holy Spirit to the minister upon the delivery of the message.

Evangelist Forrest McCullough preached in a college

chapel service one morning. He had spent all night in prayer previous to the service. When he made a call to commitment, it sounded like a flood of people responding. He had unction! One could feel the Lord talking!

The Pastor as Teacher

In Matt. 28:19-20, Jesus gives us the Great Commission for making disciples. Making disciples is not only to convince a person to make a decision to accept Christ but also to help that person learn, grow, and continually follow the Lord as a vital part of the decision. Therefore, to carry out the Great Commission, the pastor must be a teacher to help the people learn how to disciple. Jesus emphasized this truth in verse 20, that the pastor is to teach them.

How does the pastor adjust to his role as teacher? He will have to balance his ministry. A successful pastor not only preaches the Word but also teaches those new converts how to live their life in Jesus, how to share their witness, and how to teach or disciple others in the faith. If the church put into practice the slogan "Each One Teach One," the church could do so much more. The pastor teaches the believers, then each believer takes a new convert and disciples him, teaching him to disciple another.

Jesus did not use only the lecture method, which is so popular today. He also modeled for them how they were to pray, to evangelize, to know the Scripture, to use the Word, and to minister. "He led them to understand and appropriate the life and ministry of prayer in the Spirit and to be absolutely obedient to the will of God. From Him, they learned to exercise unwavering faith, to love God and man, and to work together in dedication to God's will."[1]

The goal of the pastor is to be a pattern for the people. They will watch him. They will mimic him as he follows Christ. His classroom will be in the church, at the pulpit, in a classroom setting, on the street, at home, or in another's home. Just as Christ was the disciples' Example, so Christ is the Example today also.

It has been said that it is better to show someone how to do something rather than tell him. Jesus emphasized teaching wherever He was. The place is not the important thing. The best way to teach a person to win souls to Christ includes more than just a classroom. The pastor can teach the laity and let them practice on each other. Then he can take two people with him and let them see him at work. Next they can witness as he watches and helps. That is on-the-job training. Later these experienced soul winners train others of the congregation.

The pastor is only one person. Jesus had that same problem as long as He was here in the form of man. He could be at only one location at a time, so He trained the disciples to carry His message. They trained others in turn. That is the only rapid and practical way to reach out with the gospel message.

It is not difficult for a pastor to let one of the laymen do a menial job; however, it takes more trust to watch one try to do a job the pastor can do better. Jesus trained His disciples and sent them out two by two. He watched them make their mistakes and have their failures and successes. He encouraged them to learn from those times.

We all learn more by doing than by watching. It is similar to learning a new city. I can visit a city, riding with other people, and never learn the city. When I drive, I learn the city rapidly. We all learn from doing. Jesus knew that concept very well. The pastor must put his people to work, not just sweeping the floor, but doing the ministry.

In the ministry of the apostle Paul, teaching was central. He was not only a great preacher but also a great teacher of pastors as well as believers in the churches. He was truly a disciple of all levels of the ministry. Virgil Gerber considers these elements of Paul's teaching:

1. Paul used a variety of techniques in his teaching ministry.
2. Paul had a definite content to be taught.
3. Paul was selective in his training progress.
4. Paul made Christ the center of the content taught in the churches.
5. Paul taught principles, not specific details.[2]

Never preach that your job is to be the shepherd only. You are also a sheep as a child of God. Many pastors isolate themselves from their people by creating a division between the pastor and the laity. True, the job of the laity is to win others, but it is the responsibility of the pastor as well. Lead your people! Never try to push them. That only makes them dig their heels into the ground and stop. Let them follow you as you follow Christ.

We would do well to follow Paul's model as we teach our people in the local church. In Eph. 4:11-12, the apostle Paul shares that God wants the pastor to perfect the saints for the work of the ministry. That concept is an important key for good church growth. The pastor must equip the saints to do the work of ministry! One of the most important ministries is evangelism. What would a church be like if one-half of the members worked in evangelism? The church would change! By equipping the people, the pastor begins a *system* of church growth, multiplying what he can do. Trust the laity to do the work of the ministry even if they have to learn from their mistakes.

There is a sense in which people who have extreme hurts in the physical or material realm need to have some of those hurts alleviated before they can hear the gospel. What is the responsibility of the church? To care for the whole man! The ministry in the local church must be balanced between evangelism and compassion. Many times the Haitians who live in the Dominican Republic forget their pastor's daily needs to attend to a community family in need. It is not an either/or situation. Both are responsibilities to fulfill. A pastor must train his people to care for his needs as well as the needs of the community.

The pastor will seek to have a balance of ministry to the felt needs of his people with a greater stress on the spiritual needs of the community. Many times when people get their lives straightened out with the Lord, they begin to solve their other problems of life. The church's central responsibility is to prepare people for a better life here as well as for heaven. That is only done through meeting their spiritual needs.

The Pastor as Counselor

"Preaching is the art of persuasive speaking. Counseling is the art of selective listening."[3] A minister learns to preach as well as he possibly can, and he also learns to counsel. A pastor cannot neglect this responsibility without neglecting his ministry. The New Testament idea of the ministry is the minister as shepherd. Jesus said, "I am the good shepherd, and know my sheep, and am known of mine" (John 10:14). Counseling is the work of the shepherd. The troubled are seeking help and guidance, while the minister or pastor is there to listen and advise. It is understood that he is to help all people grow spiritually closer to Christ, but counseling is an avenue of personal contact, which may be used for the maturity of the saints *and* for evangelism.

The minister is not a medical doctor and should not act like one. However, there is a strong relationship between the body and the mind. Much of the sickness of the world is not in the body but in the mind, and much of that is because of the condition of the heart. Many people today are walking around with hurt feelings because they think someone has wronged them. They cannot forgive or be forgiven. This is a serious problem. Often on a person-to-person basis the pastor can lead someone to give his hate and resentments to Christ and receive a healing for eternity. Certainly the healing of relationships goes hand in hand with the healing of hurts. Many times a person's problems are not with themselves but from strained interpersonal relationships. The pastor-counselor can learn how to deal effectively with these kinds of real problems to bring healing and restoration as well as spiritual victory. In these situations, God will give wisdom as we apply the learned skills and depend on Him.

The location for pastoral counseling does not need to be limited to the church office. The pastor can also counsel during visitation. Those who will not make the effort to find the pastor may feel free to discuss their problems when he is visiting them. The pastor can counsel almost anywhere. And, as spiritual counseling becomes more a part of his ministry, home visitation by the pastor will increase proportionally. He may leave his bed late at night to answer the distressed call of someone who wants to pray; the people know he is available and willing. However, unless he has professional training, the pastor must realize that he is not a professional counselor and may need to refer some people to professionals. If he is not careful, the majority of his time may be spent in counseling, and he may neglect other responsibilities.

Every pastor should keep records of his visits and counseling sessions. He should plan his visits and the time to be in the office to accept appointments for counseling, although there will always be emergencies and exceptions to the rule. Making a list of the different kinds of counseling he may need in his church can help the pastor organize his time and organize the laity to help. Included in the list might be:

a. Emergency cases—accidents, acute illness, death, or unusual distress

b. Chronic cases—invalids, incurables, the aged, shut-ins

c. Prospective members—including outsiders to be evangelized

d. Problems from the congregation

e. Developing pastoral qualities

Pastoral Qualities

To be effective in any kind of profession or occupation, one has to refine and develop certain characteristics or qualities. This is true in the ministry. Every pastor can develop his personality and skills to be a better minister. He can continue to learn, and he can rely on the Lord's help to be the best minister possible, even though some skills are more difficult to develop than others.

Common sense seems to be one of those traits that is difficult to learn. Common sense can be developed to some extent through learning, but it is more naturally acquired. If common sense is important for a person in the secular world, it is more important in the world of the pastor. The ability to make good decisions just through intuition and not through learned patterns of thinking is a necessity so many times in the ministry. The ability to judge situations becomes an everyday happening. Pray to the Heavenly Father for common sense to be more adept at building the kingdom of God. Some steps in decision making can be learned. Study a good book on making decisions and incorporate this into your ministry.

Attitudes are very significant for the pastor. He will be forced out of the ministry or deeper into the ministry according to his attitudes. A person with wrong attitudes has no place in the ministry. God can forgive bad attitudes and help him develop good, clean, healthy, and positive attitudes. Wrong attitudes infect people. Few are drawn to a church with negative attitudes. Healthy attitudes create a healthy atmosphere in the church. The church becomes a positive influence in the community.

Among many barriers to church growth, the attitude toward that growth is crucial.

> Congregations need to be warned against an attitude of "gradualism," which finds pastors or leaders expecting only little change or growth at any time. When leaders too quickly accept the status-quo and rationalize the difficulties and non-growth of their church, little or nothing will happen until they change their attitude and their spiritual eyes are opened to see the possibility for growth.[4]

An important characteristic of the ministry and the church is optimism—the ability to see an answer to every problem. Optimism believes that it can work. Optimism understands that God is in control of every situation. An optimistic leader finds good in all situations. A healthy outlook on life permeates throughout. Optimism is a close relative to faith.

The tragedy is that many pastors think that growth is impossible. Robert H. Schuller, who pastors the Garden Grove Community Church in California, talks about impossibility thinking.

> Impossibility thinkers are people who immediately and instinctively react to any positive suggestion with a sweeping assortment of reasons why it can't be done, or why it is a bad idea, or how someone else tried it and failed, or (and this is usually their clinching argument) how much will it cost! They are people who suffer from a perilous mental malignancy called the impossibility complex. They are problem imaginators, failure predicters, trouble visualizers,

obstacle envisioners, and exaggerated-cost-estima-
tors.

Their attitude produces doubt, stimulates fear, and generates a mental climate of pessimism and fatigue. They are worry creators, optimism deflators, confidence squelchers. The end result? Positive ideas buried, dreams smashed and projects torpedoed.[5]

The minister should be positive with people. Ministry must build people up instead of tear them down in the faith.

Being positive also affects the scope and success of the work. If the pastor thinks that something cannot be done, then it probably cannot be done. However, if the leader is positive and has faith that God will help him, then the job probably can be accomplished.

We have a good example of this from Dr. John Maxwell.

For example, a young psychology student drafted into the Army decided to test this theory. Drawing K.P., he was given the job of passing out apricots at the end of the chow line.

"You don't want apricots, do you?" he asked the first few men. Ninety percent said, "No."

Then he tried the positive approach: "You do want some apricots, don't you?" About half answered, "Uh, yeah, I'll take some."

Then he tried a third test, based on the fundamental either/or selling technique. "One dish of apricots, or two?" he asked. And in spite of the fact that most soldiers don't like Army apricots, 40 percent took two dishes and 50 percent took one![6]

The difference between success and failure is often related to a positive attitude. The "You don't really want to be a Christian, do you?" approach usually attracts fewer positive responses than "You would really like to be a Christian, right?" A positive approach nets a positive response more often than not. A minister needs to be positive in his reactions as well as his attitude. When things do not go well, as will certainly happen at times, he must react in a manner that will encourage his people to do better, rather than discourage them from trying again. Instead of scolding the latecomers, brag on the on-times. Instead of relating failures, challenge for success for the future.

There seems to be a conclusion that there are three classes of pastors.

The *progressive* pastor has an optimistic outlook on life and the ministry Christ has given to him. He does not necessarily have a large church, but usually it is a growing church. He has vision! If he is in a church that will not grow, he will not be satisfied to stay unless he can find the key to its growth.

The *maintenance* pastor intends to stay the way he is and let the church maintain itself. He does not expect the church to see great growth; he wins about the same number of people as drop out of the church. Instead of being on top of the situation and seeing the possibilities of growth, he sadly views the hard work involved and stays where he is. Usually he gets stuck with the church that wants a maintenance pastor. Sad to say, most pastors will fall into this category.

The *destructive* pastor is one who is either killing the church or is riding a dying church to the grave. He does not even maintain the church's present status. He is pessimistic about the ministry in general as well as about the problems and hopes of his particular church. If he ever had a vision, he has lost it. If he transfers to another church, it will decrease. He always puts the finger of blame on someone or something else besides himself.

What should be the relationship of the pastor to his wife?

To a certain extent the wife of every pastor will determine his level of ministry. Foremost in his ministry is his relationship to her. Can she minister at his side, or is he afraid of that? How deeply is she involved in his ministry? Every pastor must ask himself these questions.

In fact, if he is going to have a good relationship with her, then he must make her a part of his ministry! Many pastors cannot share their ministries with anyone, especially their wives. One pastor would never tell his wife where he was going or why. She felt threatened by that. Consequently, she never became involved in the leadership of the church. What wasted talent!

Another young pastor had problems when he left his wife at home all of the time with two small children. He was gone doing the "work of the pastor" while she was wondering where he was and what he was doing. Was she involved? Very little. Not only was she not a great part of his ministry, but also he was not much a part of her life. After she finally decided to leave him, he called for help, and with much counseling and prayer, he was able to adjust his ways and let her share his burden and prayer for the church. She even started visiting with him in the work of the Lord.

As the key figure for church growth, the type of pastor will determine the type of church. God condemned the shepherds of Israel who were not fulfilling their duties in Ezek. 34:1-10 and took their sheep away from them. God gave the sheep a promise to care for them in verses 11-16. The fulfillment of that promise was found in the coming of Christ, who is the great Example. "I am the good shepherd: the good shepherd giveth his life for the sheep" (John 10:11). What an example for the pastor who is the shepherd of the flock of believers!

What Do You Think?

1. What is understood by expositional preaching?

2. Why is evangelistic preaching important to the growth of the church?

3. What part does preaching play in the pastoral ministry? What part does teaching play in the Great Commission?

4. Why should the ministry of compassion go hand in hand with evangelism?

5. How does pastoral counseling tie in with church growth?

6. Compare the "progressive" pastor with the "maintenance" pastor and the "destructive" pastor. Which one do you think will promote church growth? Where do you classify yourself or your pastor? How can you better your ministry?

5

The Laity's Role in Church Growth

The pastor, if he has a growing church, is going to have a positive relationship with the people. The ministry is a people-related profession. If God has called him to be His minister, that call is to work and minister to people. If he accepted that call, then he prepares to work with people. If he is not willing to work directly with them, then he had better check with the Lord. If the pastor cannot get along with people, he had better get some help.

Many times it is said about a pastor, "He cannot preach very well, but he loves his people." Preaching is of central importance for any pastor as he strives to be the best preacher that he can be. But without love for his people, he will never be a good pastor (see 1 Corinthians 13).

The pastor of every church gets close to the people if he is to have a good ministry. He shares their heartaches as well as victories. He bears their burdens through suffering. One layman said of his pastor, "He is not the best preacher, but he hurts when I hurt." When that layman had a daughter in the hospital on the edge of death, his pastor went to the hospital and stayed all night, not saying much. His presence alone was a comfort. It is not surprising that this layman thinks so much of his pastor. The concept that Christ used was to live with His people. What would happen if every pastor took that concept to heart?

A good pastor is personally involved with his people. He must learn when to be comical and joke with them and when to be serious. No one likes to see a person who is all business all of the time. There is a balance. There is an appropriate time for joking and a time to be powerful, stern, or serious. Whatever his mood, the pastor, as God's representative, does all in love. What a challenge to the minister to find his most effective way to minister.

"When the minister begins to get restless, when he feels frustrated and ineffective, when distant pastures seem greener, he may soliloquize: 'What's the matter with me? I love the Lord, I love the Bible, I love the church, yet I seem to be getting nowhere. What's the matter?' Notice that he did not say, I love people, especially the people of this community."[1] Without love there is no ministry. Without a burden for the people there will be little drive.

What is the motivating force or strength of the ministry of the pastor? Is it to do a good job, or to be appreciated? It may be a legitimate reason like that. However, that is not adequate. The appropriate motivation comes from love for God and His work. This love is not taught or learned directly. While the pastor can teach about love, real love comes from the heart by the cleansing of the Holy Spirit. If the pastor loves his people and community, they will sense it and respond to his pastoral ministry.

Training the Laity

There is much to be done in the work of the church. Although the pastor may be trained to do the work, he must find ways to train the laity to help him. In turn, the laity will be able to train newcomers. Everyone knows that two hands are better than one. The same applies to soul winners. Two soul winners will reach more than one. Two Sunday School teachers will teach more than one.

After the people are trained to work in the church, the pastor must trust them to accomplish the work. He must not be too particular or critical if the job is not fulfilled to his exact specifications. Not only must the mature Christians be trusted, but also the new converts. Involvement of the total membership makes the church become personal. The pastor continues to supervise and guide his people, using their gifts and ideas where possible.

Unfortunately it often takes longer and is more difficult to train one to do most things than for the pastor to do them himself. He must not let himself be caught in the "busy" syndrome. Some people feel that the more they are doing, the more important and needed they are.

The pastor is an administrator among other things. He trusts his people to work in the church, and that means all types of work, not just cleaning the floor. He chooses those who have some talent and starts training them on the job, then develops others' talents and puts the whole church to work.

It has been said that the way to know if you are a leader is to turn around and look behind you. If there are people following behind you, then you are a leader. A leader should never be behind his people; they follow him. If the only way a pastor can accomplish the task of building the church is to use threats or similar tactics, little will happen. For example, when a pastor realizes that his people are not tithing, he can either preach at them negatively or be an example of the joy of giving. The latter is more apt to lead them into acceptance of giving their tithe.

As the pastor learns to lead by motivation and example, the people catch the vision of what can be done. If they are not positively motivated but are doing the work of ministry because they have to, they will quit after the pressure tactics are relaxed.

The pastor is the example. He does not ask his people to do anything he is not willing to do himself. Once I was working side by side in a church construction project with one of my laymen. After a few days of hard labor, he looked up and said, "You're different." He went on to explain that other pastors had not wanted to become involved. On the other hand, the pastor must prioritize his time and not become overworked in jobs that the laity can carry on. When he finds that balance, he is leading and administrating correctly.

The pastor always has a responsibility to the laity. That is one reason he is pastor! The beautiful biblical example of the Good Shepherd and His sheep is often used as a comparison in this situation. Responsibility is not to be confused with so-called control over the laity. One pastor thought he was called to run the church without any input from his people. The next time the church had a pastoral vote, he was looking for a new church. To properly control the church is to lead the church to make decisions voluntarily. Hopefully the pastor and the people can come together in finding the will of God for building the Kingdom. Some try to manipulate the laity, but trickery is never acceptable; divine leadership is the key.

It is important that the pastor show his appreciation to the people for all that they do for the Lord and the church. As he conveys to them his trust and love, they will feel that they are vital members of a great partnership, colaborers together.

Most people in today's world remain very quiet about spiritual things. When it comes to secular business and pleasure, they begin to talk. When the Lord's name is to be glorified, many close up again. The challenge is to mobilize the laity to share what is in their hearts. The job of the pastor is to set the pace for his laity, to show them how to do it. Training in the form of teaching and preaching as well as by example will free the laity to speak for Christ.

Involving the Laity

Some pastors seem to have the concept that if people want to work, they will volunteer or respond to an announcement from the pulpit that there is a job to be done. They expect people will run forward to participate, but this is not always the case. Many will sit back and wait for someone else to do it.

The result is that the pastor takes jobs to the laity. There is a job for everyone in the church. Find each one a job and help him look for other jobs to do. Even the new Christians are included in this process. There are many jobs they can do also. The job needs to match the talents, personalities, and gifts of the new Christians. Help each layman find his ministry.

Paul Orjala shared in a seminary class that the pastor identifies with his people even to the point of grammar usage. When he preaches, he uses "we" instead of "you" or "they." His usage includes himself. His message is not just for the listener. The goal is to influence, not to alienate. The pastor identifies with his people by becoming one of them!

"Churches fall into two extremes: *(a)* Pastor is boss, and *(b)* Members are boss. Both of these positions violate our basic structure."[2] The greatest ministry is produced when the balance of the two is found. Each situation is different. Therefore, the pastor adapts principles that will sharpen his administrative skills. Consider these basic principles:

1. Involve in decision making the people who will be involved in the implementation of those decisions.
2. Recognize that people are more important than the organization. The organization is to serve people.
3. Maintain a freedom of discussion and exchange of ideas among all groups of the church.
4. Recognize that there are no unimportant jobs in the church.
5. Recognize that there are no unimportant people in the church, that each one has a ministry to fulfill.
6. Emphasize the servanthood role of Christians—especially leaders.

7. Have a clearly recognized organizational structure with which the members are acquainted. This must include knowledge of who is responsible for making decisions, establishing priorities, and implementing decisions reached.[3]

The pastor and laymen have a partnership role of ministry that builds the church of Jesus. The pastor can do little without a congregation, and the congregation can do little without an administrator.

The special role of the pastor is to be the spiritual leader of his church. "Leadership is important because as the leaders go, so goes the church."[4] Yes, and that leadership belongs to every minister. The pastor's leadership determines, more than any other human factor, the success of the church. It is easy to get involved in running the church and have little time for preparation and the work of the ministry. The pastor is God's primary man to use in order to deliver His message of revelation. Not that God does not speak to laymen, but there are few churches where the laity rise above the spiritual level of the pastor. Time is vitally important to the pastor to develop that keen edge of spiritual maturity. There are many ways to do that, but the two best ones are to live in the Word of God and live a life of prayer.

Without a vision the pastor will not do much in building the Kingdom. To be able to see where the church is going and transfer that vision to his people is one of the primary tasks of a spiritual pastor. If he cannot see anything for the future, how will his people reach out with the message of the Lord?

With divine inspiration the pastor is like the manager of a ball team. Just like a team manager he teaches his people how to do their tasks well and leads them in practicing what they have learned. The Word is the Guide of unlimited power. It is always the Source and Foundation. Every board member is trained and challenged. Every official and layperson is a member of the team.

Developing Leadership

The principle of the pastor working himself out of a job is very important. The pastor may ask, "What am I going to do if I train someone to do all of my jobs as pastor?" That is not really the point. Once someone has been trained for a ministry in the church, the pastor can begin another task that needs to be done, and eventually he can train someone for that responsibility as well. He lets the people know that he is helping them to find their ministries. He is excited with them. As they accept their ministry and take over Kingdom-building jobs, the cycle continues. There is always something for everyone to do.

There are some areas of ministry that are especially appropriate to the laity, and some to the clergy. Many ministries are done better together by all of the people of God.

In the discussion of the ministry in the New Testament, four factors must be borne in mind: *(a)* all ministry centers in Jesus Christ; *(b)* the entire Christian community is active in ministry; *(c)* the ministry is given by God and is exercised through the spontaneous use of special gifts; and *(d)* special ministries are needed for specific situations in an evolving society.[5]

Leaders have a function as a part of the Body. They prepare others for ministry. If the Church of Jesus Christ is going to win the world, then it must have ministers. The answer is to "urge a greater acceptance of the idea that the whole church (laity and clergy) perform that ministry."[6]

The pastor will also develop pastors as he trains the laity for leadership. There is a great need for many more pastors.

In Latin America there are many Protestant congregations. Most of them have an average of at least two or three preaching points. There are many men with the pastoral gift who have been called to the ministry; however, probably not more than 90 percent have serious theological training. Even assuming that all of the students who are studying in our seminaries were to become pastors, we would still be backlogged for years in meeting the needs of filling the pulpits by conventional methods. This does not take into consideration the continued church growth that Latin America is experiencing.

In South America we have developed an Extension Education Program in the Church of the Nazarene to meet this need. We have taken the seminary to our people. In 1988 there were 2,000 studying for the ministry. For the first time in the history of this continent, we are producing enough pastors to keep up with an energetic church planting program that is netting 15-20 percent growth each year.

There probably will not be any good church growth unless a strong personality takes the lead. The pastor is the crucial one who rallies others around him. Robert Schuller wrote, "Leadership is the key to church growth. If the church is to really succeed in its mission of witnessing effectively to the non-churched world in the Twenty-First century, we must develop dynamic, aggressive and inspiring leaders."[7]

To witness is the number one task of all Christians. This is not optional for Christians. God has called His Church to the universal witness. Until the Church gets back to that universal witness, it will never make a great impact on the world. It was for that reason that Jesus said, for all Christians, "Tarry ye in the city of Jerusalem, until ye be endued with power from on high" (Luke 24:49). That power is for the believer to share his experience of salvation in the world. He is to be the salt of the earth.

An effective way to organize the body of believers to

share in witness is through directed or planned visitation. Gaines Dobbins' plan of lay care and visitation is outlined as follows:

1. Use of key persons for community oversight: division of the church community into convenient districts, with at least one devoted church family in each district charged with specific responsibility to note cases of need and opportunity, to call if possible when the occasion arises, and always to report the situation to pastor or church office. This requires no elaborate organization but appointment and continual reappointment of key persons who are willing to render this simple service.

2. Use of Sunday school officers and teachers: closer than any other lay leaders to the church's total constituency, these men and women are the logical reliance of pastor and staff for systematic and purposeful visitation. An essential aspect of their training should be in this weekday ministry of care and counseling, sometimes more significant and valuable than their Sunday services.

3. Use of men's and women's organizations: The Brotherhood and the Women's Missionary Society, or their equivalents, are usually made up of dependable and trustworthy men and women to whom the pastor may delegate certain forms of care and visitation demanding maturity, insight, patience, and skill.

4. Use of community resources: information of value may be obtained from the files of public utilities concerning newcomers and changes in residence. "Vital statistics" in the newspapers give information as to the births, marriages, deaths. Cooperation may be established with community chest agencies and with physicians and hospitals for similar mutuality of concern and service.

5. Use of visitors' cards at all regular services of the church and its agencies. Cards should be available on which names of visitors may be obtained, together with addresses and checked items indicating type of need which might be met through visit of pastor or someone else representing the church.[8]

Standards for Stewardship

The ministry of the church is developed through the stewardship of God's people. That stewardship is a stewardship of service as well as a stewardship of finances. This ministry of support applies equally to the laymen and the pastor. Together they support the complete ministry of the local church. God is concerned that both bear their responsibility.

One of their major responsibilities is to support the local church with their finances. This biblical principle that God has set up for each local church allows the members of that body to support the building of the Kingdom through tithes and offerings. Building the Kingdom is the building of the congregation, all of its outreach ministries, including the construction of a physical building.

Tithing is a biblical principle. Malachi tells us that God will open the windows of heaven and pour out His blessing upon His people who will tithe into the storehouse (Mal. 3:10). Jesus said in Matt. 23:23 that all should keep the laws but not forget to support the local church with tithes and offerings. This is a principle by which the New Testament church lived, and it is a principle by which the modern-day church lives. Without the tithes of God's people, the church will not be able to carry out the Great Commission, especially in these days of sophisticated technology and high finance.

It is vitally important to emphasize the concept of financing the church through tithes and offerings. No apology is needed from the pulpit for asserting this position. God has always built His Church this way; modern days are not exception. The minister must preach giving as every Christian's responsibility and joy. This great adventure of giving is best communicated to the people by the pastor's example. The support ministry will become a reality for everyone in the church. "Stewardship should therefore be presented not as a burdensome obligation but as glorious good news."[9]

Many pastors have taken the stand that they would not receive a person into church membership until he is a fully tithing member. That is a good principle. Unless a member supports his church, he will never completely become part of that church. When a member joyfully supports the work of God, he becomes a vital part of the Church of Jesus Christ.

The minister teaches the people that no one is too poor to tithe. God requires all Christians to be tithing Christians. In many third world countries pastors as well as laymen have felt that the poor cannot tithe. That is not biblical; even the widow gave her mite (Mark 12:42). Those who do not tithe are robbing themselves of the blessings of God.

When the laymen catch the vision of tithing faithfully and joyfully and submit to the discipline of systematic giving, then God will help them realize that "it is more blessed to give than to receive" (Acts 20:35). As they grow in grace they will "seek . . . first the kingdom of God, and his righteousness" (Matt. 6:33). The pastor must be the one to teach the biblical principle of tithing in his church. However, he must also teach the joy of giving above the tithe. Tithing is the beginning. It is well known that the president of Colgate-Palmolive makes it a practice to give nine-tenths to the Lord, and he lives on the one-tenth.

Lay Pastors

In addition to supporting the work of the ministry, many times the laity will perform the work of the ministry, even being called on to preach or even pastor an extension of the local church. Some people have the erroneous idea that one cannot preach the Word of God unless he has a call of God to be a pastor. In Acts chapter 8, Philip, a layman, went to Samaria and there preached the gospel of Jesus Christ. Philip not only preached the gospel, but he baptized those believers too.

When the apostles in Jerusalem heard that the Samaritans had received the Word of God, they sent Peter and John. When Peter and John arrived, they prayed for the new converts to be filled with the Holy Spirit. A mighty revival is recorded in Acts 8 because Philip, a layman, was obedient to God and preached the Word. He did the work of the ministry. Laymen can preach the Word.

Every layman will not have the call to be a pastor. However, there are natural leaders in every church. It is the role of the pastor to identify and cultivate those natural leaders. After teaching them how to preach and how to do the work of the ministry, the church sends them out. How thrilling it would be if every church could have from 10 to 20 different extensions pastored by lay pastors. Some may eventually study in colleges and seminaries.

The ministry of the senior pastor in his local church could be multiplied in effectiveness if he has a nucleus of lay pastors who minister also. Their ministry extends his ministry. What a concept for the local church. What a concept for the role of the laity—to be God's lay pastor. He may never receive the credentials of ordination, but he can preach the Word of God and do the work of ministry. He may never have a call of God to be a full-time pastor, but he can fulfill God's call to witness to his faith. At the same time, his ministry benefits the local church while extending the work of the local pastor.

Although the role of lay pastor is not for every Christian, there is one role that every born-again believer can have—one ministry that all Christians can develop—the ministry of encouragement. Gus Bergesen, a layman friend said, "I do not have a lot of talents. However, God has given me one ministry: that is, to encourage others in the faith." How easy to fulfill, and how great a result and effect it has on other people. Encouraging new Christians to continue in the faith, to believe more of God, to mature in the love of Christ encourages the brethren to become more active and involved in the ministry. How rewarding it is to hear words of encouragement from each other. Everyone needs encouragement. Encouragement may be just a word or two of appreciation to build confidence. God will multiply the ministry of encouragement. Barnabas encouraged Paul to continue the work of the ministry. (See Acts 9:27-31.) He was willing to work with him. Pastors can build this kind of ministry with the laymen.

Big Brothers

The church has the idea of the "come" ministry. People are expected to "come" to the church without any invitation from the local congregation. The church needs a "go" ministry. If the church will "go" and invite and win, the people will "come."

When people finally do come to the church and are converted, are they told to "come back next week!" as they leave on Sunday night? Do they live in the cold, secular world for a whole week without any Christian nurturing, education, or help?

No one would ever think of taking a woman to the hospital to give birth to her child, and then the next day after the child is born, put it out on the front step and say, "There is the world; live it up." No, that is not the way to raise a child. The child will be nurtured, fed, and helped for many years until he can live in the world by himself.

That same care should govern our treatment of new

Christians as well. The "Big Brother" concept pairs a mature Christian with a new Christian. It is understood that the pastor trains the Big Brothers to do their jobs. The pastor should not place someone in this responsibility unless he is sufficiently trained or is training on the job. The Big Brother concept works only as well as the training emphasizes the nurture and help new Christians need to mature and grow.

The Big Brother could go every night for the first few days and talk to the new convert to encourage him, give him strength, and help him to grow in grace. A Big Brother has many responsibilities. He helps a new Christian make choices and establish priorities. He tries to keep him from choosing to go back into sin. He gives him moral encouragement to make the right decisions. He stands by him if he falls. He prays for and with him. The Big Brother sees that he comes to church and studies the Bible. The Big Brother can lead the new Christian in a converts' class of Bible study.

Using this system of follow-up ensures conservation and growth of new believers. The pastor may oversee a program like this, or he could put someone in charge of it. The organization could have training sessions with the Big Brothers as well as sessions with the new believers from time to time. Big Brothers should report regularly to the pastor. He will advise them about how to handle difficult problems that seem to have no solutions.

The Big Brother is actually in charge of the new Christian and is responsible for the nurturing and growth of the new believer in Jesus Christ. How many more converts could be saved for the church if this plan were implemented? This follow-up system has the added feature of giving the people the feeling that God is using them in the ministry of building the Church of Jesus Christ.

If a believer cannot make the intense commitment to be a Big Brother, he can pray. All believers can pray not only for their own spiritual lives but also for the services of the church. Frequently Christians go to church without praying for the services. When this happens, how can the services be much more than form? If the believers in the local church would unite in faith, pray, and believe that God would do something in their services, what tremendous power there would be in the services of the church. Every believer should go to church expecting God to do something special.

If all Christians were praying that God would give them new converts, new people would be born into the kingdom of God during the services. The power of the church lies in this concept! Teach the people to pray for all Christians, as well as for the new Christians. Pray for the outreach program of the church; pray for the complete ministry of the local church.

Another aspect of prayer centers around altar work. The people need to know how to work at the altar. Most of the time the pastor, and only the pastor, prays with new people or members at the altar. The whole congregation sits and watches from their seats. The pastor can expand his ministry by teaching laymen how to win people, how to bring people to faith, and how to counsel at the altar. While the pastor is giving an altar call for unbelievers to come forward to accept Jesus Christ or to pray for a need, the laymen, one by one, should accompany them to the front. While seekers are praying, the altar worker's presence renders encouragement. When the seeker runs into a problem and does not know how to continue, the altar worker would be able to lead him in prayer. Altar workers provide vital assistance to new or struggling people as they come to the knowledge of Christ and His perfect will for them.

The Work of the Ministry

In Eph. 4:11-16, the apostle Paul gives the scope of the ministry. He declares in verse 11 that the Lord chose some to be apostles, prophets, evangelists, pastors, and teachers. Their job as leaders is to perfect the saints for the work of the ministry and to edify the Body of Christ—to bring the Body of Christ into the unity of the faith that each one in the church may know the Son of God and be brought into the fullness of Christ. What does the apostle Paul mean by perfecting the saints for the work of the ministry? He is saying that the role of the laity is to prepare to do the work of the ministry. Who will teach the laity to do the work of the ministry? It falls back on the pastor. He is to help the whole body of Christ to find the ministry that God wants for each person.

When this happens, the body of Christ is not "tossed to and fro, and carried about with every wind of doctrine" (v. 14). The minister needs to teach the people what the Word of God says because there are many influences and forces working to undermine the body's faith.

The church needs builders. There is no place in the church for someone who is going to wreck it, destroy its reputation, or to change it from the will of God. The Early Church believed that service and leadership went together. As the Church grew, it seemed that they needed to share the responsibility for church management. In Acts 6, the apostles began to realize that they could not carry on the ministry of prayer and preaching the Word if they had to continue to minister to the needy. When they realized that that ministry could be accomplished by the laypeople, they chose laymen to carry out the building of the Kingdom. As the laymen shared in the apostles' responsibility, the Church could continue its effective ministry, "the word of God increased; and the number of the disciples multiplied in Jerusalem greatly" (v. 7). This could only happen because of joint ministry.

In this passage of Scripture we see the characteristics of

those laymen who were chosen. We are confident that these should be the characteristics of all leaders of the church today. First, the apostles chose leaders who had wisdom. This is a necessity. The church will not be built with leaders who lack wisdom. What is *wisdom?*

One Bible translation explains this characteristic as "practical common sense." This requirement means an obligation to think hard; to discover productive solutions for the work of God. It is not the wisdom of the world, but the will of his Lord which he seeks. This trait makes the Christian leader know that the church depends utterly on God. He wants to know clearly the difference between presumption and achieving faith.[10]

Second, they were full of the Holy Spirit. Indeed, every church leader must possess this characteristic. How can a leader lead unless God's Spirit is with him? He needs His divine hand leading and guiding him. Being *full of the Holy Spirit* means that the leaders had received God's Holy Spirit in the cleansing, sanctifying experience, empowering them for service. Equipped for service, their witness will be effective, not frustrated. That was what the Early Church expected. Complete dependence on the leadership of the Holy Spirit was the distinctive of the Early Church.

Finally, the chosen laymen were well respected. What does *good reputation* mean? Everyone thought well of the leaders. They were respected as lay leaders, and the community of faith looked up to them. Their achievements and dependability resulted in places of natural leadership. The apostles expected them to have a good reputation and be a positive force in building an effective church.

Every Christian is responsible to have a changed life. His daily relationships must be open and honest. He treats his fellowman as Christ would treat him. He strives for the common good of the people. Together with the pastor he seeks to bring people into the perfect will of God. This kind of leader will enjoy a wide influence on all of the other members of the body as well as the local community—a tremendous asset in the building of the Church of Jesus Christ.

What did these lay leaders achieve? What was their job? Was it to tell everyone about Jesus Christ? Not necessarily. Really, their job was more of practical service. As they were obedient and served others, God began to use them to tell others about Christ. Stephen, persecuted and martyred, influenced others as he testified of the grace of God in his life. According to chapter 8 of the Book of Acts, Philip went to the Samaritans where he preached the Word of God, and great revival came. In the same way laymen in the church today can be God's active, living witnesses.

What Do You Think?

1. What part does love play in church growth? Where does this love come from?

2. What is understood by saying that love delegates and trusts?

3. What does it mean to guide or direct by motivating by example?

4. What is the difference between making the laymen responsible and controlling them?

5. What is meant by mobilizing the laymen?

6. How are the pastor and laymen partners?

7. What are some of the best ways that the pastor shows spiritual maturity? Why?

8. What does the expression "the pastor works himself out of a job" mean?

9. Explain the concept that both the laymen and pastor carry out the ministry.

10. How can a layman preach the Word to fulfill the work of the ministry? What is understood by the term *lay preacher?*

11. Explain the meaning of the ministry of "going."

12. Explain Eph. 4:11-16 in relation to the extension of the Christian ministry.

13. What were the characteristics of the laymen chosen for service in Acts 6? Explain them.

6

The Growing Church
(A Model)

Every pastor will have something to do if the church grows. No one starts a church and then expects it to grow on its own. Like a gardener he keeps the weeds out, nurtures the new plants, and helps them come to maturity.

First, develop church growth eyes. On the surface this looks like a strange statement. When a farmer looks at a field ready to plant, he can see the harvest ahead. A pastor with church growth eyes will be able to see the potential in the church. He can see possibilities to make the church grow. He collects the data and analyzes it in order to make a conclusion. That conclusion will aid him to develop a growing church.

Second, there is no one formula for church growth. It would be nice to have a pat answer and say, "If you pray, plan, and work in a certain manner, you will have growth." The formula for church growth is not one-sided but many-faceted, since what works in one place may not work in another. The pastor will need to choose, even by trial and error, the best system of church growth for his situation. As regional director for South America, it has been necessary to use some of the same church growth principles but customize them in the different districts.

Most important, a strategy that allows church growth cannot be just on paper. It must be in the heart, and the pastor's passion must be communicated to the people. It must possess a dynamic and motivating force provided through the leadership of the Holy Spirit.

A particular method that works in one situation may be completely wrong or difficult to use in another area. The methods need to be culturally adapted to the people. Any church growth concept must fit the situation and become a part of the people. Using concepts foreign to the culture without adjusting for differences is being completely insensitive and will not work. The pastor may borrow ideas from any place in the world, but it has to become a part of him in order to fit his local situation. As an example, in Latin America lady pastors are not well accepted because of the role of women in the culture.

The pastor who is growing his church must seek the guidance of the Holy Spirit and plan for the church to grow. He chooses a plan for his situation. Sometimes he may have to follow an alternative to that plan. Then he must be willing to let God change the plan or program for growing the church. Sometimes He intervenes and moves the pastor in another direction. Church growth does not always happen the way the pastor wants it to happen. Many times God has a better way to do things. At times the Lord closes the door to our plans, only to open a much better door. After all, He sees the total picture for growth in all situations. The pastor in the final analysis must say, "Lord, it is Your church. I submit my plan to You. You change it and direct it any way that You wish."

"Leadership, faith, and goal-setting are intertwined in the attitudes and actions of a growing church."[1] The result of a vision is accomplished through goal-setting and planning. Goals must become an important part of our strategy of building the church. Goals are set in the area of evangelism, for it is the heart of church growth. The pastor needs to set definite goals or numbers, as well as establish a time limit, if the church is to fulfill its purpose to its membership and its community. Missionary Ted Hughes taught me the importance of numbers. He asked, "What is the difference between 30 and 31 members or converts? If No. 31 were my son, it would be very important." Goals and numbers are important! The following goals can be set:

STRUCTURE
    organization (to perform effectively)
    personnel and staff requirements
    site and facilities (whenever appropriate)

SPIRITUAL MINISTRY
    worship (corporate)
    personal ministry to members (edification)
    education (of all ages)
    fellowship (among members)

DISCIPLESHIP
    stewardship (of abilities and financial gifts)
    lay leadership development
    outreach and evangelism
    social ministries[2]

Ken Carney graduated from the Nazarene Bible College and took a pastorate in Columbus, Ohio. He was told that the community could not be reached around the church and that the church should be moved. God gave Ken and his church a vision. Running about 100 in attendance, they set a goal to have 300 in attendance in six months. Vacation Bible School and canvasing the neighborhood provided 200 new contacts for their church. Exciting things began to happen. In a period of six months they had 290 people in church. A month later their goal was 400. They had 390 people in their church service. God has blessed them. This changed the image of the church in the community, and it has continued as a strong church, ministering to the needs of the area.

A widespread plan used today in extending the church is the satellite model. Many movements and growing churches around the world are expanding and extending their church by means of the parent church. A parent church can parent several different satellite churches at the same time, which multiplies the number of areas where people can "enter" the church. Satellite churches also multiply the number of people and the number of leaders, thus expanding the influence and ministry of the parent church. This concept is very successful in South America. Antonio Correa in Buenos Aires has 25 satellite groups. His church has grown to a capacity of 500 members. Now he is planning to organize new congregations with some of them.

Satellite churches come in a variety of types. There is the cottage prayer meeting, where several members of the parent church hold a prayer meeting, in another community. Or there is the home Bible study, in which someone from the parent church teaches a week-by-week Bible study. After the pastor has had a training session each week, he sends the leaders out, working along with them on the job also.

The circle of concern is usually geographically designed. A lay leader is given the responsibility of church members and interested contacts who live near him. They may meet on a regular basis for Bible study or fellowship. The lay leader must report regularly to the pastor. The pastor should be notified of any emergencies involving those families. The lay leader follows up on Sunday School absentees. Those in the circle of concern know that they can contact him for help at any time.

Eventually many satellite groups will become regular churches with a local preacher or a lay preacher from the parent church actually pastoring the congregation. They may even have their own building.

The advantages of the satellite structure are that they provide visibility, develop leaders, and start new churches. New people can actually see the church in action. The more people involved in the ministry of the church, the more the church will accomplish. The leaders will have accountability to the mother church and to the senior pastor as he supervises them. The expansion of the mother church in developing a daughter church will result in the formal organization of a new church at a later date as it grows. Until that daughter church is organized, those members will be a part of the mother church, which increases its numbers and finances.

Satellite plans like these are possibilities that can work in any part of the world. Most of the growing Churches of the Nazarene in the Dominican Republic have two or more extensions. Cho in Korea has successfully used this plan to build his great church. The Methodist Pentecostal church in Santiago, Chile, using this model, has 80,000 members.

Pastor Dario Tello has set as a goal to start a daughter church each year from the Mapasingue Church of the Nazarene in Guayaquil, Ecuador. He has done this, and now many of the daughter churches are reproducing, making Mapasingue a grandmother church!

In Peru, the Church of the Nazarene has been spread throughout the country by "moving Nazarenes." When a member is transferred to another city, if there is no church, he begins the church in his home. Usually the mother church will help with some visiting leadership, depending on the distances.

In four years, the Church of the Nazarene in Venezuela has grown rapidly. In the beginning of the work, a few churches were started in strategic cities, then those churches became the mother churches to extend the church in that region of the country.

Through the use of satellite churches and other church growth methods we are winning the world for Christ because we are fulfilling the Great Commission to make disciples. God helps us with more ideas or strategies to keep on doing His will.

What Do You Think?

1. What does the phrase "to have church growth eyes" mean?

2. Why is there not one formula for church growth?

3. Explain the phrase: "Leadership, faith, and establishing goals form an intimate part of church growth."

4. What do goals have to do with church growth?

5. Explain the "satellite model" as it pertains to church growth.

Conclusion

Church growth is more than a strategy—it is a way of life. It is just as natural for the church to grow as it is for one to breathe. One of the parables of Jesus about the Kingdom speaks about the spontaneity of church growth:

> The kingdom of God is like a man who casts seed upon the soil; and goes to bed at night and gets up by day, and the seed sprouts up and grows—how, he himself does not know. The soil produces crops by itself; first the blade, then the head, then the mature grain in the head. But when the crop permits, he immediately puts in the sickle, because the harvest has come *(Mark 4:26-29, NASB)*.

This parable speaks about the mystery of church growth. That mystery lies in the potentiality of the seed. During the germinal stage of the Word of God, the seed is acting in each believer. Each believer multiplies himself by spreading the seed of the gospel. The seed has inner force, its potential. This parable invites us to discover the potential that is in each of us to make the church grow. The Word of God has a lively, efficient, irresistible force. The Kingdom is the power of God, not the action of man. The sower does his work; the seed depends on him to be spread out. However, the power is in the seed. The seed does not receive the power from the sower, but its power is contained within itself.

Once the sower does his work, he lets the seed work itself. The sower must let the seed do its part, "to let it work," and sometimes this is the hardest thing for us to do. The Christian is not a builder of the Kingdom, and less a programmer or director of the work. He is a person that offers possibilities for growth, spreading the seed.

It seems that the key sentence in the parable is "how, he

himself does not know." Here we see the big smile of God over our church. We must have His plan for our church. We must spread the seed and let it grow. The sower in the parable does his work well. That is our part.

While the pastor creates favorable conditions for church growth and attends to church growth strategies and philosophies, if he depends only on these, he will miss having real growth. This comes only through the divine Spirit of God. Out of a growing church will come several things.

1. Leadership will be developed among the laymen who minister in the local church, and God will call others to go into new areas to build His Church.

2. Replication, unlimited repetition, is the purpose of every leader—duplication of himself, and then by the process of replication, he can be duplicated over and over and over again. Material items, such as power amplifiers, cannot be replicated. If the pastor is dependent on *things* in order to duplicate and multiply the church's growth, then there will never be multiplication. Replication in the church only takes place when many people share the gospel of Jesus Christ continuously. Others then can go into the world to tell other people.

3. A movement is the result of the multiplication of members and churches.

If the pastor is really planting a church with the correct base, he will preach and demand complete obedience to God in everything, including tithing, not to help the pastor financially, but because it is part of the plan of the gospel of Jesus Christ as well. A growing church has a good financial base.

At their fifth assembly in the Dominican Republic the church had an 80 percent increase in local church financing. That means the Dominicans were concerned that their church grow. They believed in the biblical emphasis of tithing and giving of offerings into the church.

One pastor came to me as his district leader and asked for a raise. What did I do? Did I give him a $50.00 raise? No, I said, "Go back to your church, win some new people to Jesus Christ, teach them to tithe, and you will have your raise."

It is of utmost importance that the pastor organize himself and his church for growth. He needs to take a good look at himself. What is his purpose? Why is he pastoring this congregation? What can God do to work through him to build His Church? As he begins to organize himself and his church, he will develop strategies and plans. He will involve the people in these planning sessions. He may want to get several books and study church growth strategies and principles. Certainly he will want to study his community as well as his church. He must base his strategies and plans upon the personality of his church and his community. Then he will begin to work the plan.

What will you, the pastor, do next? What will you do with these concepts? As you start the process of building the kingdom of God:

1. Admit your failures. It is not necessary to make excuses. You can admit that you are not doing all that you can. That is true even if you are doing a lot in the church. No one is doing all that is possible. You must be ready to face up to your shortcomings.

2. Be open and ready to change. If you can learn something from someone else, take advantage of that opportunity.

3. Develop the details of a plan. A plan in general is not sufficient.

4. Preach for the moving of God upon the people. God wants to build His Church.

5. Minister to the people and their needs. Help them grow and find their ministries.

6. Have a personal desire to grow. Have spiritual as well as numerical growth in the church. The church is always one generation away from extinction. It is imperative that it grow. God wants to help. Growth creates more growth.

I am excited to be part of God's team in helping souls find Christ and become established in the church where a pastor and trained people will extend the ministry of the hand of God to their community and beyond.

Endnotes

Chapter 1

1. See Gen. 12:2; 18:18; 22:18; Pss. 96:10; 102:15; Isa. 2:2; 54:3; 60:3; Jer. 7:28; Ezek. 36:23; 39:21; Joel 3:2; Mal. 3:9; etc.

2. Waldo J. Werning, *Vision and Strategy for Church Growth* (Chicago: Moody Press, 1977), 19.

3. Paul Orjala, *Get Ready to Grow: A Strategy for Local Church Growth* (Kansas City: Beacon Hill Press of Kansas City, 1978), 37.

4. Werning, *Visions and Strategy,* 26.

5. Orjala, *Get Ready to Grow,* 34.

6. Elmer L. Towns, *The Ten Largest Sunday Schools and What Makes Them Grow* (Grand Rapids: Baker Book House, 1969), 118.

7. George Peters, "A Missions Program That Succeeds," *Action* (Summer 1975), 12.

Chapter 2

1. Dean M. Kelly, *Why Conservative Churches Are Growing* (New York: Harper and Row, 1972), 121.

2. Bennett Dudney, *Planning for Church Growth* (Kansas City: Beacon Hill Press of Kansas City, 1970), 23.

3. Orjala, *Get Ready to Grow,* 86.

4. Donald A. McGavran, *Understanding Church Growth* (Grand Rapids: Wm. B. Eerdmans Publishing Co., 1980), 341.

5. Orjala, *Get Ready to Grow,* 97.

6. Elmer L. Towns, John N. Vaughan, and David J. Steifert, *The Complete Book of Church Growth* (Wheaton, Ill.: Tyndale House Publishers, 1981), 281.

7. Ibid., 35-36.

8. Orjala, *Get Ready to Grow,* 23-24.

Chapter 3

1. Lee Lebsack, *Ten at the Top: How 10 of America's Largest Assemblies of God Churches Grew* (Stowe, Ohio: New Hope Press, 1974), 94.

2. Towns, Vaughan, and Steifert, *Church Growth,* 19.

3. Orjala, *Get Ready to Grow,* 51.

4. Dudney, *Planning for Church Growth,* 92.

5. Virgil Gerber, *Discipling Through Theological Education by Extension* (Chicago: Moody Press, 1980), 36-37.

Chapter 4

1. Gerber, *Discipling Through TEE,* 106.
2. Ibid., 110-15.
3. Gaines S. Dobbins, *A Ministering Church* (Nashville: Broadman Press, 1960), 154.
4. Werning, *Vision and Strategy,* 56.
5. Robert H. Schuller, *Move Ahead with Possibility Thinking* (New York: Doubleday and Co., 1967), 14-15.
6. John C. Maxwell, *Your Attitude: Key to Success* (San Bernardino, Calif.: Here's Life Publishers, 1984), 106-7.

Chapter 5

1. Dobbins, *Ministering Church,* 169.
2. Dudney, *Planting for Church Growth,* 53.
3. Ibid., 54.
4. Towns, Vaughan, and Steifert, *Church Growth,* 35.
5. Erwin L. Lueker, *Change and the Church* (Waco, Tex.: Word, 1976), 162.
6. Gerber, *Discipling Through TEE,* 144.
7. Robert H. Schuller, *Your Church Has Real Possibilities* (Glendale, Calif.: Regal, 1974), 14-15.
8. Dobbins, *Ministering Church,* 159-60.
9. Ibid., 144.
10. Neil B. Wiseman, *Leadership: A Leadership Development Strategy Manual for Church Growth* (Kansas City: Beacon Hill Press of Kansas City, 1979), 37-38.

Chapter 6

1. Towns, Vaughan, and Steifert, *Church Growth,* 209.
2. Werning, *Vision and Strategy,* 50.